Leading Your Association Through an Economic Downturn

an ASAE Background Kit

asae | american society of association executives

American Society of Association Executives
1575 I Street, NW
Washington, DC 20005-1103
Phone: (202) 626-2723; (888) 950-2723 outside the metropolitan Washington, DC area
Fax: (202) 408-9633
E-mail: books@asaenet.org
ASAE's core purpose is to advance the value of voluntary associations to society and to support the professionalism of the individuals who lead them.

Ann I. Mahoney, CAE, Vice President, Knowledge and Content Management
Anna Nunan, Director of Book Publishing
Glenda Beal, Acquisitions Coordinator
Jennifer Moon, Production Manager

Project management by Susan Doran.

Cover design by Design Consultants and interior design by K Art & Design.

This book is available at a special discount when ordered in bulk quantities. For information, contact the ASAE Member Service Center at (202) 371-0940.

A complete catalog of titles is available on the ASAE Web site at www.asaenet.org/bookstore

10 9 8 7 6 5 4 3 2 1

Contents

Preface

Leading Your Association Through an Economic Downturn is a new background kit that compiles the latest information about how associations faced with dwindling budgets are dealing with the challenge to deliver quality service to members.

The selected information spans the years 1999 to 2002 and is reprinted from ASSOCIATION MANAGEMENT, several American Society of Association Executives (ASAE) newsletters, and other relevant ASAE and non-ASAE sources.

Leading Your Association Through an Economic Downturn includes information on financial management, staffing issues, membership recruitment and retention, marketing and advertising, and meetings. It also contains sections on cost-saving tips and case studies.

Introduction

Dealing With the Economic Downturn

By Gerry Romano, CAE

Reprinted from
ASSOCIATION
MANAGEMENT,
November 2001

Wouldn't it have been wonderful if by the time this article rolled off the press its theme was yesterday's news? Unfortunately, despite the interest rate cuts by the Federal Reserve Board and the economic stimulus package winding its way through Congress, it will still be awhile before the economy pulls itself out of this slump. That's bad news in general, yet—as is often the case—the association community is finding ways to address the negatives while taking positive steps.

Some executives describe ways in which they've restructured operations. While the efforts began in reaction to economic ultrachallenges, the positive results have proven the value of periodic reevaluation, whether times are easy or rough.

Some executives go on to explain ways in which their associations are not only surviving but growing stronger in today's unfriendly financial environment by upping the member-service level. They focus on a concept worth keeping in mind while the economy remains worrisome: Members need their associations more than ever during difficult times. "If your members are facing a severe downturn, ask yourself what products or services your association can provide to help," advises financial consultant Andrew Lang, executive director of BDO Seidman's National Center for Excellence in Nonprofit Management, Bethesda, Maryland. (For details from Lang, "Big-Picture Perspective and Advice," p. 8.)

Whether reworking the association's apparatus or developing new member benefits—or both—executives are taking constructive steps while the economy takes a nap.

Pathologists association reviews, revises, and revamps

Extensive restructuring has been the American Society of Clinical Pathologists (ASCP) response to the problematic economy. Based in Chicago, ASCP has reorganized the society, centralized services, trained staff on new technology, and developed partnerships.

ASCP members—80,000 pathologists, served by ASCP's staff of 145—began to feel strains from the economy a few years ago, says chief operating officer Louis Apostol, CAE, but the subsequent impact on the society has varied. There have been no membership declines, for example. "Growth has come from our associate members, and technologists are beginning to see the value in belonging to the society," Apostol explains. But, like other association executives quoted in this article, ASCP has seen a decline in educational program participation, although associate members are participating.

"We've had flat revenue for the past three years—we've had revenue increases in some areas but not others. Educational programs, attendance at national meetings, and sales of special publications are down," Apostol says. On the plus side, however, advertising revenues for ASCP's two journals are picking up.

Commenting on the impact of the slowing economy on ASCP members, Apostol shares a common refrain. "Our membership has grown, even though the economy has sputtered. The area where we're starting to see sliding, however, is in members traveling to our various programs. Previously, monies in members' budgets were allocated for this, but budget cuts at hospitals and other facilities where our members work have affected travel."

ASCP took on the tough economic challenges and effected some changes that show that, sometimes, drastic times call for drastic measures. ASCP contracted with Deloitte & Touche in 2000 for a management study. "They developed a list of initiatives that we undertook," Apostol says. "We reorganized the society, and now we have more of a horizontal management structure rather than vertical. We broke down silos. We established intradepartmental operations and activities. And we centralized all services—such as marketing, financial services, and operating services, which we consolidated into one department. Now different divisions work together on multiple projects."

These kinds of changes are not without challenges, though. ASCP faced several, Apostol says, including changing the former paradigm, in which division heads operated only their teams and were not involved in other teams; retraining of staff; and completely automating the office. "From a technology standpoint, we improved each area, which facilitated a lot of the changes and the integration of services," Apostol notes. However, more challenges surfaced, as the staff needed training on the new technology—a big project—and ASCP felt the need to downsize.

"We looked at how people were doing their jobs and reevaluated, spreading activities into multiple parts—centralizing is one aspect, project sharing in another," says Apostol. "The educational programs are involved in the business services group, marketing, and so forth.

"I set up four work process groups," he continues. "One is an internal research and development process group to work with a research and development committee in developing projects and business opportunities for the society. Another is a customer-service, work-process group. Plus there's an information technology work process group that looks at the integration of technology throughout the society and external volunteer process committee to look at how we can better use volunteers."

Sharing the work has extended outside ASCP to include academia and other associations. "Our research and development committee established a relationship with a university to allow members to sign up for courses and get college credit. We also have projects in distance learning—we work with a vendor to offer courses for people who can't attend our meetings," Apostol says.

He also mentions new, joint programs currently being planned with the American Association for Clinical Chemistry, Washington, D.C., and the Clinical Laboratory Management Association, Wayne, Pennsylvania. "These programs are mutually beneficial," Apostol says. "These organizations are looking at having a meeting that involves many different disciplines, and ASCP is doing a series of workshops with them to expand opportunities for our membership."

Partnership plans continue: ASCP is launching a corporate development program to get corporations more active in the society, such as by sponsoring workshops and programs. "We're going to do a study of what the corporations can do for us while they get more visibility," Apostol says.

In addition, ASCP is reevaluating its volunteer structure. "We pay for volunteer travel," says Apostol, "but the biggest challenge is for volunteers to find time outside their jobs to volunteer."

ASCP's changes are in place for the long term, not just as short-term fixes, Apostol emphasizes. "Even if our revenue increases, we'll keep all these changes in place. It's just good business practice to do so.

"Change is very difficult," Apostol comments. "It scares a lot of people. It has to be handled well; it can't be imposing. But change means change: People need to understand that there will be streamlining and that technology can displace staff, hopefully through a normal attrition."

In orchestrating ASCP's strategies for dealing with the economic downturn and taking the association into the future, Apostol has attempted to apply best practices from corporations. "Not many associations are on the cutting edge; a lot of cutting edge comes from the corporate world, which looks at the bottom line," he says. "Associations are not for profit; but keep in mind," he urges colleagues, "we're not for loss, either."

Tough times for IT in general

The 500 corporate members of the 38-staff Information Technology Association of America (ITAA), Arlington, Virginia, are "undergoing a lot of stress right now," says ITAA's chief staff executive, president Harris Miller. "Our companies have had a dramatic slowdown in growth or, in some cases, a drop in sales.

"Feedback from our member companies about the impact of the economy came in late 2000, even though the slowdown started earlier," Miller says. "In terms of membership, even though we've lost a lot of companies because they're no longer in business, or they cut expenses to the point where they no longer can pay association membership dues, we are seeing a substantial overall growth in membership this year," he says. "We expect to see double-digit growth in membership dues, because companies still want to join."

The decline for ITAA has been "on the nondues revenue side, particularly at our conferences and other events, as well as in sponsorships and other types of programs," Miller says. "There have been dramatic changes in terms of revenue compared to our original projections," he comments, based on the fact that money from members' marketing budgets—to participate in sponsorships, for example—and money for staff travel to events has been decreased. "Companies continue to join the association, and they participate," Miller says. "But when it comes to sponsoring a booth at an event or sending an attendee to a conference, that's not happening as much," he notes.

To compensate, ITAA has cut back spending, and, according to Miller, is "searching for other nondues revenue sources and for ways to continue to grow

our dues revenue, which is our major source of revenue." But, he acknowledges, "There's no magic bullet here."

Miller accepts that the economic slowdown is not over yet. "I'm planning on it lasting through at least next year. I assume that monies from companies' marketing budgets and travel budgets will still be frozen through at least much of 2002."

Rough road for human resources

Talk about tough: During an economic slump, human resources professionals are prone to be hit when they're down. After the stress of overseeing company layoffs, HR managers may find that their own jobs have been eliminated.

Judy Weil, CAE, executive director, Northeast Human Resources Association (NEHRA), Wellesley, Massachusetts, tells how the turmoil has translated into an opportunity for NEHRA to demonstrate its dedication to service as well as build loyalty among members. In June, the association launched Members in Transition, a free program offering NEHRA's 4,000 members career transition seminars, coaching in interviewing skills, advice for negotiating salary and severance packages, facilitated networking meetings, access to databases, free resume posting on NEHRA's Web site, and other career assistance—plus a one-year membership dues waiver. By partnering with local outplacement firms to provide this program and serving as a vehicle to bring the expertise of these firms to HR professionals in need, NEHRA is able to provide its members with critical help while strengthening the bond between members and service providers. "We had people signing on for this program the minute they heard about it," says Weil. "It took off like wildfire."

Weil has words of advice for association colleagues no matter the economic state but especially during hard times: "Be creative. Be proactive. See an opportunity and think about what resources you have to create programs to fulfill needs.

"I think of this as sort of the golden age of associations," she continues. "Employees no longer assume that their employer is going to look out for them and provide for their long-term career needs; instead, they need to be responsible for their own. That's where associations come in. Associations have the ability to fill that void and to provide what all professionals need, which are skills and knowledge and networks. And here we are in that perfect position to provide all of those things."

In spite of the severe economic slowdown, Weil reports minimal decline in NEHRA membership and educational program participation. She lauds the generosity of about 15 supplier organizations whose support made it possible for more than 30 members to attend NEHRA's annual convention, which was held in early November at the Rhode Island Convention Center in Providence, for free. But she also stresses that members fully realize the importance of staying involved.

"Individuals are recognizing that if you're responsible for yourself, you're not going to stop building the capacity that you need to be successful just because you are temporarily between jobs. So an enlightened view of the long term, and acknowledgement of the importance of continuing to be on top of the latest and greatest techniques and knowledge, push individuals to continue to gather those skills."

Economy takes a toll on tooling and machining

The 2,430 companies that make up the National Tooling and Machining Association (NTMA), Fort Washington, Maryland, create dies and molds—the equipment that forms the products made by manufacturers. And, as NTMA president Matt Coffey, who leads a staff of 30, puts it, manufacturing has been "going south." Thus, his members, who serve the wide range of manufacturing industries, entered "a recession environment" last fall. Coffey notes that although some segments of manufacturing are still doing well—the portable

power generator business, for example, thanks to the energy crisis—"overall, there's been a dramatic decline in the amount of work that is available."

Those declines naturally led to a decline in membership for NTMA. They also led to association reengineering. "This downturn really caught us in the middle of a business planning cycle," Coffey says. "We have been re-engineering our association for the third time in the 15 years I've been here. We see such dramatic global trends occurring in the business, that we have to keep adjusting the association to keep it central and vital to the membership.

"The most important thing that I've been doing," Coffey says, "is talking with owners and advising them on ways in which they can change their business model, because the older systems that they had grown up with no longer work. The Internet has created a global market, therefore they are now competing with everyone around the world, whereas they used to just compete with the guy down the street. So we're taking people through a very aggressive program of updating their information technology as well as their production technology."

To do so, Coffey has conducted a series of lectures, traveling to various parts of the country and inviting members to learn about redesigning business to stay in sync with current trends. Plus, NTMA delivered a four-day presentation at its annual meeting on making a tooling and machining company better, faster, and cheaper.

These initiatives are reflective of an overall shift in NTMA's educational offerings. "In times like these," Coffey says, "the education needed becomes much more specific to each company. Members call us because they've got a problem, and we attempt to talk them through their problem and give them counsel on how they might approach the market, how they might rearrange their finances, how they might reposition their company, how they might upgrade their technology."

Coffey reports that the hardest hit that NTMA has taken from the economic downturn has been in textbook sales. "We have 13,000 customers for our textbooks, and our sales are off 60 percent in one year. It is a phenomenon of the community colleges not being able to get the enrollment, and the employers drawing in because they don't want to be spending money when they don't have orders very far beyond the horizon."

The shrink in nondues revenues during a short period of time has caused NTMA "to tighten up things around here," says Coffey. "We are cutting travel, for example, and trying to conserve resources so that we can minimize any potential losses we're going to have for this year."

Meanwhile, and quite significantly—and perhaps surprisingly—NTMA is "taking kind of a counterintuitive approach to this downturn," notes Coffey. "Our subsidiaries have substantial reserves, so we are considering borrowing money from the subsidiaries for the main association, which the main association will have to pay back to the subsidiaries as we get through this process."

According to Coffey, the association is going through an International Standards Organization (ISO) certification process. It requires looking at every process of the association to make sure each one supports the goals, objectives, values, mission, and vision of the organization as formulated during its strategic business planning. During this year and next, Coffey anticipates "making a major investment to build staff and build the organization...through which we will substantially lower our costs and further improve our productivity. We believe that the association is going to wind up better, faster, and cheaper—just like our members need to be. And we are going through this international certification program because our members are being forced to go through it by their customers. We feel that if they're feeling the pain, we ought to be feeling the pain as well, and in doing that, we'll have a much better association going forward."

Coffey advises other association executives to follow suit: "It's the kind of investment in the future you've got to make even in a downturn, because you don't want to hunker down too much and miss your opportunity to make major improvements in the way you deliver services to your customers."

Restaurant association membership gets a boost

The National Restaurant Association (NRA), Washington, D.C., is experiencing record membership growth and record retention right now, and what might be the most interesting aspect of this trend is that NRA's growth is not despite the economic slowdown, but rather because of it. Senior vice president of membership Michael Johnson theorizes: "People join us for help with business solutions. Sometimes a little bit of down current, if you will, is good. History has shown that people join associations during two times—panic and euphoria—and they don't do anything during status quo. Times such as the energy crisis or a time of worker shortages prove to be reasons why people join."

NRA's staff of 250 is fielding many requests for assistance from its 235,500 members. "When people are watching their financial resources or are becoming more conscious of their customer accounts and so forth, they're calling us for help," Johnson says. "Products that address issues such as 'how to increase my check average,' 'how to increase frequency,' and 'how to work with the staff I have' are examples of requested solutions. A negative situation has created positive growth, because people are looking to us for solutions to keep ahead of the curve."

Johnson says that the slowing economy has affected NRA members in that "restaurant operators who are staying successful, who are staying above the fray, are getting back to basics. They're making sure that they're treating their regular customers as well as possible, because when business travel slows down a bit or some companies aren't doing the same amount of entertaining, operators want to make sure that their current customers—their bread and butter—are well taken care of."

NRA members in some geographic areas are feeling a bigger pinch from decreases in business travel and business dining budgets. "Operators in certain parts of the country—for example, the Bay area in California—have had a drop off," Johnson reports. "When you look at an area that has had incredible growth, such as Silicon Valley, it may be a case of readjusting to the times."

Slowdowns at truck stops and travel plazas

About 1,100 truck stop and travel plaza operators belong to NATSO, Inc., Alexandria, Virginia, along with 260 allied members. They started to feel the impact of the economic downturn about a year ago and in two distinct ways, according to Lisa Mullings, vice president of public affairs.

"First, our members are consolidating," Mullings explains. "A lot of the bigger guys are buying up some of the smaller guys, so we haven't lost that many members in terms of locations, but we have lost members in terms of number of corporate members involved in the association.

"Also, our members are buying fuel at higher prices because of the higher fuel prices and, therefore, are needing to charge their customers higher prices," she adds. "So truckers—especially those who are independent—are having a difficult time; they have increased costs but are not seeing any increased income. Truckers have to buy fuel, but they need to cut back in other areas, so our members are seeing less in terms of sales in their stores and restaurants."

The trickle-down effect has been lower attendance at NATSO events. "Last year was disappointing for us in terms of our trade show, but we were in Los Angeles—a new venue for us—and most of our members are in the eastern half of the country," Mullings points out. "I think that had a lot to do with it. Our members always had a difficult time pulling away from work and keeping their facilities staffed, but they had a particularly hard time going as far as Los Angeles." NATSO's upcoming show will be in Nashville, where Mullings anticipates an increase in attendance.

NATSO has made significant changes based on current economic conditions. "We're doing some new things," Mullings says. "This year, in an effort to try to get more of the members to visit the exhibitors, we're not charging for our trade show. And we're greatly reducing the registration fees for the convention so it's more affordable." Mullings admits, "We really haven't done a great job of marketing the show in the past, and we developed a marketing plan this year in an effort to get more of our members there."

NATSO has made organizational changes, too. "We cut our budget this past year—mostly due to the stock market plunge—and we cut our staff back by two, which was a lot for us, as we're only a 20-person staff. We outsourced part of the convention, and all our departments had to cut their budgets by 15–20 percent to reduce costs."

Mullings remains optimistic despite these difficult days. "Our members have gone through cycles during the past 10–15 years, and we've been around for more than 40 years. We will continue to offer our core services," she assures. "We will overcome this."

Business slow for IT event managers

The Computer Event Marketing Association (CEMA), Sudbury, Massachusetts, began a career-assistance initiative in May. Any of CEMA's 635 members—event managers for information technology companies and suppliers of event services—affected by corporate downsizing can take advantage of the Bridge Program for help in bridging the gap between jobs. Networking opportunities, job postings, and career outplacement resources are offered in addition to a four-month membership extension.

CEMA executive director Trinette Cunningham articulates the wide-ranging effects of the economy on all CEMA members, even when jobs are not lost. "Some of our members have scaled down their events, while other members have eliminated events all together. Event managers at IT companies have travel freezes that prevent them from attending our annual event.

"That's where we see the effect of the economy from the association perspective," Cunningham continues. "Our membership numbers are up, our retention numbers are up, but attendance at meetings is down because of the travel freezes. Also, our sponsorships are down this year, and sponsorships were a huge nondues revenue source for us. Last year our sponsors were eager just to get their name out there, but now they want to make sure that the return on investment from that sponsorship is extremely high."

CEMA's overall response to the economic impact has been broad. The association, which employs 3.5 staff and outsources work to six individuals, is reviewing all outsourcing contracts. Cunningham points out that while she wants to make sure that CEMA is getting the most for every dollar spent, "I want to make sure that we don't decrease the value of membership in our association. I don't want to save money if it means cutting the value of membership in the association."

CEMA also has been reviewing the format of its educational programming.

Cunningham explains what she calls "tweaks" to CEMA's calendar of events. "We usually have four face-to-face educational workshops in addition to our annual conference. We have to examine this further, but we're probably going more to webcasting seminars instead of face-to-face, because that will save people the travel costs: They can just enroll and turn on their computers."

Overall, Cunningham believes that now's the time "to make sure our members know that we're really there for them. If we're going to do any new programs, now's the time to do it, because they'll get noticed. Anyone can join an association when the money's coming in, but the current environment is one in which we need to beef up membership programs.

"The economy has made us look at ourselves and ask: If I were a prospective member, would I join CEMA? If not, why? We have to bring more value into the association," Cunningham says. "The economy has really made us examine the association, and we've grown because of it."

She believes that within CEMA's experience are lessons applicable to other organizations. "If an association is weak, it will become weaker in this economy," Cunningham asserts. "But if it's strong, it will become stronger."

Reprinted from

ASSOCIATION

MANAGEMENT,

November 2001

Big-Picture Perspective and Advice

To get a broad perspective on the impact of the economic slowdown on the association community, ASSOCIATION MANAGEMENT turned to Andrew Lang, executive director of BDO Seidman's National Center for Excellence in Nonprofit Management, Bethesda, Maryland, a management consulting and certified public accounting firm that provides financial services to more than 300 national associations. Lang is a frequent writer and speaker on how associations can maximize dues plus develop alternative revenue streams.

ASSOCIATION MANAGEMENT: How is the current economic environment affecting membership numbers?

Lang: Associations in general are working hard to maintain membership levels, but the organizations that do a great job filling their members' needs are still growing.

ASSOCIATION MANAGEMENT: What are you seeing in levels of educational program participation?

Lang: A noticeable decline in the sale of education products—especially meetings and seminars. During hard times, education is one of the first things to suffer in an association budget.

ASSOCIATION MANAGEMENT: How are sales of other types of products being affected?

Lang: There is certainly a decline in sales of higher-dollar items for those industries hardest hit by the economic decline. Where a major vendor might previously have bought four contiguous booths, now that vendor might only buy two or three in a row. Smaller products, such as books, are generally still being purchased, though.

ASSOCIATION MANAGEMENT: How have you seen associations respond to the declines?

Lang: Most that have economic troubles are cutting costs however they can. The intelligent ones target specific items within the various activity areas. Less insightful associa-

tions cut some percentage, say 10 percent, across the board. Some of the worst-hit entities have had to cut out all but core activities. Many associations are looking hard for alternate revenue streams through such things as adding advertisements, exhibitors, or sponsors; adding low-cost, high-interest Internet-audio seminars; and identifying royalty opportunities.

Most associations should take the opportunity to reassess the pricing of existing products and services. It is all too common for associations to consider the direct cost of a product or activity—such as the cost to print a book—but to forget the overhead costs. If prices are not based on the full cost, the association could believe it is selling a product at a profit when it is actually selling it at a loss. If the product or service is selling at a loss, there are three considerations: Can you raise the price? Should you sell at a loss? Or should you drop the product or service?

Another consideration is that of outsourcing. If an activity is highly cyclical—such as biweekly payroll or annual meeting staffing—money likely can be saved by outsourcing. This strategy has been employed by many associations in better economic times, but it is coming into its own in the current climate.

The times require that associations think of themselves as the businesses that they are. Associations can and do fail. Entrepreneurial thinking is called for today. There is no mission without a profit margin.

ASSOCIATION MANAGEMENT: What other advice do you have for executives?

Lang: Drop any product or service that is no longer valid. This is one of the best opportunities you will have to do so. Blame it on the economy. Alternatively, if only a few members benefit from something on which you are losing money, raise the price far enough to at least break even. If members won't pay the break-even price, drop the product or service.

ASSOCIATION MANAGEMENT: What is the biggest challenge you've seen an association face in dealing with the economic downturn?

Lang: Perhaps the worst I have seen is where an association had to determine its core programs and then shrink to the core. This requires letting programs go, which makes members unhappy, and letting staff go. There are no easy answers to this dilemma. The best thing to do is to keep the mission firmly in mind and do what will be best for the majority of the members. It is better to do less than to no longer be able to do anything at all.

Financial Management

Of Belt Tightening and Bullet Biting: Strategies for Surviving Uncertain Times

By Robert J. Cocchiaro, CPA

Reprinted from
Dollars & Cents,
ASAE newsletter,
March 2002

Across the past year we have witnessed significant declines in the stock market, rising unemployment, terrorist attacks, and attempts to prop up our economy by the Federal Reserve through numerous interest rate cuts.

Some organizations have received significant contributions for victim assistance programs and similar activities. Other organizations have seen funding reductions from private foundations (with reduced distributions as a result of a weak market), reduced membership receipts as members seek more value for their membership dollar, and some redirection of charitable giving as a result of the events of September 11, 2001.

In October 2001, Raffa & Associates, P.C., held a workshop, "Weathering Funding Reductions," which brought together leadership from 70 nonprofit organizations and asked them to collaborate around a central question: "How will giving be impacted across time by the current realities, and how will my organization be impacted directly?" The result of this workshop was the identification of several fundamental strategies from nonprofit organizational leaders who have experienced past crises or navigated their organizations through uncertain times.

1. **Focus on your core mission and strengths.** Your organization's financial resources should be expended on activities that are *mission critical,* activities that support what the organization was established to do. Bring the board and staff together to refocus their efforts around the mission. Identify the organization's activities (programs, products, members

services), evaluate them against the mission, and decide if it's worthwhile to spend valuable financial and human resources on activities that don't further the organization's mission.

Enact an almost ruthless prioritization of activities in order to focus on what is critical in achieving the mission. Strengths and weaknesses must be reviewed even when carrying out mission-critical activities. If there is another organization that is better at delivering the service or program, consider partnering or transferring the entire program to it. The reverse is also true. Determine what your organization is best at and focus on or expand that area by shifting resources. What is important are outcomes and long-term survival.

You also should be on the look out for *mission creep,* pet projects from board members or staff that do not necessarily further the organization's mission. Some of these drain financial resources while many others are *silent killers,* which require few direct dollars but take up valuable staff time.

2. **Develop a realistic contingency plan.** Take a hard look at your organization's situation, and identify and evaluate your risks from reduced funding. Review the major sources of revenue, assessing which are most likely to be impacted and by how much. This may involve contacting major funders and reviewing historical trends. With this information, plan for the best, most likely, and worst-case scenarios for your organi-

zation, and develop strategies to deal with each one. Make the hard decisions now so that you can react quickly to any crises. Create a budget or financial plan for each scenario, and identify what expenses you can curtail or delay while delivering on your mission.

If you are confident that your risk is minimal, begin developing a contingency plan by establishing an operating reserve and annually contributing to it. If your organization is fortunate enough to already have a reasonable reserve, consider using it—wisely.

3. **Drive resource development and build capacity in key areas.** Times of economic uncertainty demand aggressive fundraising efforts. Don't be afraid to ask for donations of money or time. Target those who have given before. Focus on your organization's outcomes and accomplishments when fundraising. Don't just tell potential donors how much you need to raise, show them what you have done in the past and what you will do tomorrow. Increase volunteer recruitment efforts to leverage your financial resources.

4. **Establish or enhance strategic partnerships.** Foster open lines of communication with organizations that are complementary to your association's mission. Find a common ground, and focus on identifying overlaps, strengths, and weaknesses. For example, consider co-hosting a meeting or conference or partnering to carry out social programs.

5. **Manage costs.** Organizations can curtail expenses without eliminating entire programs, activities, or people. Avoid across-the-board expense or staff reductions. These tactics may work temporarily, but they are not long-term solutions because they do not consider the organization's ability

to deliver on its mission. Focus on the following areas:

- **Financial information** is the most critical piece of datum you will need to manage your costs. You must know the true costs of each of your programs and activities and how your actual revenue and expenses compare to your budget.

- **Eliminate or delay unnecessary expenses** such as travel, entertainment, and training. Look for ways to accomplish the same results for less.

- **Delay purchases of capital assets** (furniture and equipment) as long as they don't negatively affect your mission-critical activities.

- **Monitor your cash flow** daily and keep an updated cash-flow projection to identify potential shortfalls. Give priority to paying the bills that are critical to your organization. If you do not have a line of credit, consider getting one while your organization is financially healthy.

- **Review vendor contracts** for supplies and other items to make sure you are getting the most competitive prices. Get competitive bids.

- **Program reductions** should be among the last steps when additional cutbacks are necessary. Start with nonmission-critical programs. If an activity does not support your mission you probably shouldn't be doing it. Evaluate and consider curtailing the impact and cost of less-mission-critical activities. Eliminating or reducing programs is difficult, but remember, if the organization is gone, it can't help anyone.

6. **Open the lines of communication, and protect trusted relationships.** Communicate changes in situation frequently and openly with your staff, board, funders, donors, and suppliers. Ask for the same open communication from them, especially in regard to potential funding reductions. New

relationships with donors and funders take time to establish. Focus on existing relationships and building trust with these stakeholders. Engage donors in other capacities (volunteering) to expand relationships in nonfinancial areas. Communicate what your organization is accomplishing in order to anchor their support.

There are no definitive answers for navigating uncertain times—only experience-based strategies that will help your organization make the right choices. These strategies are at the core of sound financial management during good times. They are even more critical during uncertain ones.

Reprinted from
Dollars & Cents,
ASAE newsletter,
February 2002

From the Listserver: Surviving Tough Times

Finance & Administration Section
Council members monitor all of
ASAE's section e-mail lists to respond to
finance-related questions and to share
responses or comments that section members may find of interest.

Question:

Given our current economic times, I am
wondering what other organizations are
doing to avert deficits such as pay cuts, layoffs, forced vacations, and so forth.

—**Al Hamwright,** *vice president, finance
and administration, Community
Associations Institute, Alexandria, Virginia*

Response:

We are identifying financial triggers and
then planning how we would respond if
they occur. We will be reevaluating plans on
a quarterly basis. Our goal is to avoid layoffs
if possible. Our initial contingency plan
includes a hiring freeze, reducing staff and
volunteer travel, and reevaluating project
priorities.

We also have the luxury of a fund balance
that is around 100 percent of one year's
expenses, which gives us some breathing
room.

—**Rebecca Garris Perry,** *senior vice presi-
dent of operations and CFO, American
Health Information Management
Association, Chicago*

Response:

Here at the Food and Drug Law
Institute, we are certainly feeling the effects
of the economic downturn. We have just
gone through a major restructuring that
resulted in the loss of three positions (five
people out, two new people in). We will
probably not be giving raises or bonuses this
year. We have frozen capital spending, and

we are cutting all nonessential expenses.
Even with all of this we are still worried
about the future. I would be interested in
hearing what others are doing to try and
survive the next few months.

—**Carol Gavin,** *director of finance and
administration, Food and Drug Law
Institute, Washington, D.C.*

Response:

It is too early in our year to determine
the impact on us. I would only caution that
whatever actions you take, try not to endan-
ger the basic programs that you have in
place. Things will turn around, and it will
become difficult to hire good people again.
If you have strong reserves, this is the time,
possibly, to dip into that rainy-day fund.

—**Robert R. Goyette,** *director of finance
and administration, Massachusetts Bar
Association, Boston*

Response:

In the past year we have worked to significantly lower our expenses. This became
even more of a priority toward the end of
2000 as we saw our advertising and sponsorship revenues begin to be affected by the
economy. We revised our budget in May
2001 (we are on a calendar fiscal year) based
on a revised forecast of revenue that was
down $500,000 from our original projec-
tions. Below I've listed the major cost items
addressed and how much money we've been
able to save.

- Outsourced three functions that had
  been done in-house, which saves us
  approximately $160,000 a year. These
  functions were customer service, circu-
  lation processing for our two magazines, and a print competition that is
  held for our members each year.

- Hired new auditors, which saved us
  approximately $15,000 from what our

previous auditors were charging.

- Renegotiated our phone and Internet services, including local, long-distance, and T-1 charges, which saved $15,000 a year.

- Stopped using a lockbox and now have employees process incoming checks for deposit. This is saving us $15,000 a year.

- Renegotiated our credit card merchant fees and saved $10,000 a year.

- Combined membership renewal packet materials onto a CD-ROM that is sent to members. This enables us to send them much more information then we ever could have on paper, and it has saved $20,000 a year.

- Reevaluated our insurance risks and needs and saved $10,000 a year.

- Renegotiated legal fees on an indemnification program (errors and omissions) we offer to members. We decided to bring the legal function in-house, but when we presented this to our attorneys, they were willing to reduce their fees. This has saved us $150,000 a year.

- Reevaluated a magazine that we publish that has been losing money for years but that was funded because it represented the future of photography (digital). We recently decided to close the magazine, but when we discussed this decision with our printer, he offered to print the magazine for $8,000 less per month. When we combined this with publishing the magazine bimonthly instead of monthly, we were able to save $140,000 a year, which was enough to allow us to continue publishing the magazine.

The total of these savings alone is more than $500,000. Because of these measures, we are projecting higher fund balance increases in 2001 and 2002 than we've ever produced as an association, despite the economic downturn. Going through this process has taught us that we didn't know what was possible until we tried. The last two items alone are proof that cost-cutting efforts can produce very unexpected results. To find these savings, though, we have to be willing to question everything and not be afraid of change.

I've realized one more thing as we've gone through this process. All the ideas have come from our senior managers, primarily our executive staff. One of our goals in 2002 is to tap the ideas and creativity of the rest of the staff as we continue to look for ways to improve our bottom line. I highly recommend *Profit Building: Cutting Costs Without Cutting People,* by Perry J. Ludy (Berrett-Koehler, 2000), for those of you who are going through, or need to go through, this process.

Scott Kurkian, CFO, *Professional Photographes of America, Inc., Atlanta*

Reprinted from

ASSOCIATION

MANAGEMENT,

April 2002

CEO to CEO: In Light of the Current Economy, How Have You Revised Your Financial Strategies?

Our organization is a bit of an anomaly in the current economy. Education in disaster recovery and business continuity is the core of our mission; thus, we are seeing increased demand for our educational courses in these fields in light of the events of September 11, 2001. Where we are experiencing a downturn, however, is in registrations for our public courses around the country. This has caused us to place much more emphasis on providing in-house courses to insurance companies, high-tech companies, financial institutions, and so forth. This shift in our marketing is yielding significant benefits, both for the organization (in terms of increased profit margins) and for our instructors, who are more readily available for private consulting.

Thomas C. Mawson, *CAE, Executive Director, Disaster Recovery Institute International, Falls Church, Virginia*

Living in the fastest growing county in Tennessee affords us a strong real estate economy. Our leadership is consistently conservative—and yet proactive—with the members' money. Part of that fiscal responsibility involves constantly monitoring the services offered. We are working more closely to identify membership needs through focus groups, thereby maintaining the viable services and discontinuing those that are no longer applicable to member needs.

Our association is looking at some alternative ways to raise funds through the use of technology. Our members are going to need a better understanding of technology and a presence on the Web. We are looking at pro-

viding a menu of services that will be nominal in costs to members but will create better marketing and branding opportunities for them.

Helen Carter, *CAE, Chief Executive Officer, Williamson County Association of Realtors, Franklin, Tennessee*

We are fortunate to have fairly diverse revenue streams, which gives us some flexibility in the current market. Nevertheless, we continue to seek out appropriate revenue opportunities that we believe will return more revenue than expense invested. While we are not dependent on investment income for our operating budget, our chief financial officer and our outside investment counsel had the foresight to begin reducing our noncash holdings many months prior to September 11 and the economic downturn. Our continuing strategies are to watch revenue-generating program performance very closely; pay greater attention to the word on the street in our industry; seek cost savings at every possible turn; and refine our budgeted expense contingency plans.

Kevin B. McCray, *CAE, Executive Director, National Ground Water Association, Westerville, Ohio*

We have experienced a downturn in revenue due to the national recession, the September 11 events, and a downturn in the assisted-living industry due to overcapacity. On the national level, we have focused on our revenue-generating ideas—membership, conferences, magazine advertising, sponsorships, and the sales of products and services—based on a theme of "when the going gets tough, we do a lot of marketing." This means a temporary shift of resources from areas that do not generate revenue. Invaluable to us has been the active participation of our board members, who roll up their sleeves and call peers to join or renew memberships, join our leadership council, and become industry partners.

Jeanne P. Luschin, *President and Chief Executive Officer, Assisted Living Federation of America, Fairfax, Virginia*

We had to look seriously at both expected revenues and the expenses of serving the membership in today's economy. Our budgeting had to be conservative, since the revenue expectations for our retailer members was shaky. We took an aggressive approach: We increased our dues, which had not changed since 1988, and made expense reductions in all areas that would be invisible to members. The staff looked at our typical expenses and discovered significant savings in office supply and daily maintenance costs. We then cut expenses in ways that have no visible effect on our external audiences.

William H. Baxter, *CAE, President and Chief Executive Officer, Retail Merchants Association of Greater Richmond, Virginia*

Budgeting 101

By Lorili Toth, CAE

Reprinted from
Membership
Developments,
ASAE newsletter,
June 2001

The word *budget* often strikes fear into a manager's heart. Yet, with a few deep breaths and four simple precepts, creating and maintaining the membership department's budget can be just another task for the membership manager.

1. **Budgets include revenue and expenses.** There must be enough revenue to offset expenses to ensure that the association continues its services to members. In developing a budget, both sides of the equation—revenue and expenses—must be projected. It should also be noted that even not-for-profit organizations can (and should) generate enough revenue to have a positive cash flow. Excess revenue (called *profits* in the for-profit world) can be placed in reserves for future use. Reserves are maintained to help protect the organization against hard times, prepare for expansion, or to fund special projects. The organization's tax advantages will be maintained as long as reserves are justified and not excessive.

2. **The budget is a financial representation of the plan.** This precept provides the easiest way to remember what pieces go into the budget.

   • What are you planning on doing in that budget cycle?

   • How much will it cost?

   • How much money will it bring into the association?

   Each activity—administrative, marketing, or operational—should be outlined and have appropriate dollar amounts attached to it. Without some idea of the activities to be conducted during the year, there is no starting point for creating the budget.

3. **The budget is only a guide.** As plans change for the department or the association, so will the revenue and expenses. The most basic example of changed plans equaling changing finances is membership renewal mailings. If you budgeted for three mailings, but members renew on the first one, then your plan to mail two more renewal notices should change. This should result in a change in the budget, too, at least to the bottom line, as you will save money by not sending the second and third mailings.

   The budget is there to guide you throughout the year, not tie your hands. It should be flexible enough to allow you to modify your action or marketing plan to accomplish your goals. These changes may mean halting one project to do another or reducing the expenses toward one activity to increase another. Times change, and because most budgets are done in advance of the actual budget cycle, sometimes it is necessary to modify actions or expenses to accomplish the department's or association's goals.

   Although there must be flexibility, budget numbers remain the same throughout the cycle for use as a benchmark in helping you determine if you are under or over budget. That leads directly into the final precept.

4. **Monitor your budget and use *actuals* for future reference.** This will make future budgeting efforts easier. If your finance department provides monthly reports of your area's revenue and expenses, check them against your records. If there is a difference in coding or posting, make a note of it and talk with your finance staff. When the next budget time comes around, you'll have a realistic picture of whether the previous

budget was over- or underestimated. For example, if you budgeted $9,000 on lapsed-member surveys and the actuals reflect only $4,000 spent, you need to re-examine how the numbers were established.

Although specific activities will depend on the association's membership goals, the basic activities that membership professionals should consider for their budgets are dues, renewal, recruitment, retention, staffing, and services.

How to create a budget

To create the budget, get estimates or bids on all aspects (copywriting, design, printing, postage, etc.) of the various activities (renewal notices, recruitment promotions, new-member kits, database upgrades, etc.) projected for the upcoming year. In addition, consider if you will need to expand staff or if there are new services to be offered. Again, take the time to review the actual expenses from the previous budget cycle and use them as a guide to ensure that the proposed budget activities are in line with actual expenses.

This also is the time to consider adding, dropping, or modifying activities—if a project was unsuccessful, don't include it in the budget. It is not advised that you take the

previous year's budget and increase it by an inflation percentage. This will only come close to being a realistic budget if:

1. there are no new activities for the year,
2. all costs increase at the same percentage, and
3. your previous year's budget was completely accurate with your expenses and revenue.

Developing realistic expenses for each activity may take time, but it will provide a more accurate picture of what your department will spend on projects.

Generally speaking, the largest portion of a membership department's income will be dues revenue. Projecting membership growth and therefore dues revenue involves growth and attrition trend analysis, knowledge of the potential member universe, and crystal ball reading. To establish a realistic dues revenue number, you must first project a realistic membership growth and attrition number for each membership dues category—then do the math.

Each organization has a budget format and process. Line items, account numbers, spreadsheets, and activities will vary. What shouldn't vary is the desire to provide an accurate, realistic, and actionable set of numbers for the department's budget.

Reprinted from
ASSOCIATION
MANAGEMENT,
May 2002

In Reserve: Emerging Strong Out of a Weak Economy

By Carl Levesque

With the longest period of economic expansion in history fueling it, the stock market surged ever higher during the 1990s, dovetailing with the Internet-centered, infinite optimism of the time. As investment consultants repeatedly told us to pour our savings into equity-heavy 401(k) accounts for long-term growth, it follows that in this frenzied climate some associations might have rethought their traditionally conservative reserve investment strategies of CDs and fixed income in favor of ones emphasizing equities. Why not reap some of the returns of the New Economy? During that time, in fact, ASSOCIATION MANAGEMENT, in its June 1998 issue, chronicled how one association increased its investment returns by 200 percent across a 12-month period by revising its conservative investment strategy (see "A 1990s Investment Success Story Revisited," see p. 157).

Three years and one recession later, have associations rethought those strategies yet again? Were associations, like many individual investors, a little too optimistic in their handling of their reserves? The examination of three organizations, in addition to the association covered in the article on page 157, reveal how the recession affected their operations, their reserves, and, most important, their investment strategies going forward.

Perhaps as intriguing as the three organizations' investment strategies are their varying views of the purposes and uses of their reserves. Some associations view reserves exactly as what the term suggests: a pure rainy-day fund. Other associations have a much more flexible view of how reserves are to be used, actually factoring reserve earnings into their annual operating budgets. Of most significance, however, are the commonalities that the organizations share: All have significant holdings in equities, all have

in place a written investment strategy, and for the most part all are sticking with their current strategies—generally asserting that they have no regrets in spite of an off year or two.

A rainy day arrives

American Physical Therapy Association (APTA), Alexandria, Virginia, is a classic example of an association that has been challenged financially during the past few years. In addition to the economic downturn taking its usual toll, the association's members were hit by the effects of federal legislation that cut down on Medicare and Medicaid payments that they were eligible to receive. As is usually the case, when members were affected economically, so was the association.

APTA takes somewhat of a traditional approach to its reserves, considering them as rainy-day funds to be dipped into only when times are tough. However, the association cannot be viewed as tight-fisted with its nest egg, for it has shown during the past few years that it will not hesitate to dip into its reserves when that rainy day does hit. After all, that's what they are there for.

"There has to be an acknowledgement, and that takes a political commitment, if you will, to say that if you do build up a reserve, there has to be a willingness to use it," says Chuck Martin, CAE, senior vice president, finance and administration for APTA. "Otherwise, the reserve will just keep getting bigger and bigger. And so I congratulate our elected leadership that they have had a willingness to use the reserve, and secondly, that they haven't put unreasonable pressures to slash and burn when we've had the resources [in reserve] to do what we're supposed to do for members."

APTA could financially afford to fulfill its mission of advocacy and maintain its member services because it had built up a nest egg of reserves that allowed it to do so. The association, which has a budget of $24 million for 2002, aims to keep a reserve within a range of 40–55 percent of its annual operating budget.

Always with an eye on the long term, APTA emphasizes diversification. Its investment strategy starts with two separate funds that are controlled by different entities: 20 percent of the association's reserves are in index mutual funds, which the association itself monitors, and the other 80 percent are invested by Fiduciary Management Associates (FMA), Chicago.

For the mutual fund assets, the association maintains a 60–40 equity-to-fixed-income balance. Those funds are rebalanced annually to maintain that ratio.

The association, however, gives FMA a much wider range of flexibility for the assets it manages: Those assets have an 80–20 range—in either direction. "This is almost like no restriction," acknowledges Martin. "They can swing on their own [with the 80–20 rule], stocks to bonds or bonds to stocks. In other words, we don't want them to be 100 percent [invested] in anything, but the 80–20 gives them a heck of a lot of flexibility." Granted, APTA puts other restrictions on FMA by way of its investment policy, which establishes limits on stock purchases of any specific company, minimum ratings for bonds, and so forth. So while the investment policy is flexible, it is also comprehensive.

While APTA's reserves experienced losses in 2000 and 2001, Martin notes that over the long term the portfolio has performed well. "In the decade of the 1990s we basically [maintained our] current investment policy, and we were budgeting at a 10 percent return, and most years we were well above that," he points out.

Reserves as operating funds

For the National Association of College and University Attorneys (NACUA), Washington, D.C., the term *reserves* means something entirely different from APTA's

rainy-day interpretation. In fact, that term could be viewed as only partially accurate, for the association's spending policy, which is part of its overall investment policy, allows it to regularly withdraw up to 7 percent from its reserves to support its annual operating budget, which is $2.3 million. "That is based on the premise that you are using earnings, interest, and dividends only as a payout and you're not dipping into the principal of your investment," says Paul Parsons, deputy CEO at NACUA. "The payout is used to support general operations."

Parsons, however, notes that his association has moved to lower the payout to 3 percent to preserve its reserve level given the downturn in the market value of its investment portfolio during the past year. While its reserves have declined during the past year, the association itself remains on solid footing, thanks to a strong membership retention rate of 97 percent and other stable nondues revenue sources. Still, NACUA did not ignore the economic downturn. After September 11, 2001, it created what Parsons calls a "worse-case-scenario budget" and explored measures that it might have to take if its March meeting and June annual meeting experienced severe attendance drops. Fortunately for the association, it doesn't look as though it will have to turn to the alternative budget. Nevertheless, Parsons views the development of the budget alternatives as a learning experience. "I'm very glad we did it because it was a very educational exercise," he says. "And I highly recommend that others do that."

One policy issue that the association was grappling with at press time was the level of reserves it will maintain relative to the operating budget. "That is the key question at the moment," Parsons says, adding that staff planned to recommend to the board that the association maintain reserves of at least six months of operating expenses, with any funds beyond nine months free for consideration "for future strategic initiatives."

In spite of NACUA not having such a policy yet, Parsons stressed its importance—especially in light of the association's regular use of the funds for its budget. "What's key is to define how much you should always maintain in reserves so that you don't constantly find yourself dipping into your investments—because they'll be gone before you know it," he says.

NACUA's investment strategy, which Parsons says took more than a year to develop before being adopted in 1999, calls for equity investments to stay within the range of 40–70 percent of the portfolio, and for fixed income to remain between 25 and 50 percent. The association separates cash and cash equivalents from its fixed income category, maintaining a 5–15 percent range for them. Within the equity category, NACUA has a 20 percent cap on international securities. It rebalances its assets annually to meet all ranges. Management of its funds are also diversified: Its funds are divided among seven individual money managers held through Olcott Consulting Group at Prudential Securities, Vienna, Virginia.

NACUA's reserves did lose value recently. In light of this performance, is Parsons contemplating changing course? "I think the key is to stay diversified," he says. "As long as you're mindful of the need to rebalance and as long as you monitor the performance of your individual managers you should stay the course."

Beating the bear market—by accident

The Eugene and Agnes E. Meyer Foundation, Washington, D.C., has no income except for its investment earnings. "We don't sell anything, we don't have memberships," points out Kristen Conte, vice president for finance and administration for the foundation. What the foundation does have, though, is an endowment of $150 million.

Still, the foundation must find a way not only to feed its annual operating budget of $1.5–$2 million. It also is vested with the daunting mission of doling out more funds each year in grants than it did the previous year—whether the stock market happens to be up or down. The foundation has been

successful at that goal every year since its incorporation in 1944. (It gave about $9 million in 2001.)

It should come as no surprise that a $150 million organization has an investment strategy that is reviewed regularly: The foundation revisits its strategy formally every two years. "This organization has seen the value of being very explicit in its objectives and handling its funds in a way that meets those objectives," says Conte.

At the moment, the foundation's range for equity is wide—40–80 percent of its portfolio—but that will change soon. That is partially due to its new investment managers, Cambridge Associates, Arlington, Virginia, having advised the foundation that the range is *too* wide. No final decision has been made, but Conte believes the lower end of the range will be bumped up, while the 80 percent ceiling will remain as is. Real estate is also included in the equities category. The fixed income category, meanwhile, stands at 20–40 percent.

Ironically, of the four organizations covered in this article and in "A 1990s Investment Success Story Revisited" (see p. 157), the one that was the most successful with its investments through the recession is making the most changes to its strategy going forward. While most investors painfully watched their portfolio values plummet in 2001, Conte's foundation finished the year at a highly unusual *positive* 8.1 percent. Conte and associates, therefore, must be patting themselves on the back, right? Wrong. The foundation is extremely grateful for what happened, but the impressive results, she readily admits, happened by accident.

As it turned out, the foundation's fixed income holdings, already on the high end of its limit when the downturn began, kept performing well, further skewing the ratio of fixed income to equities. In addition, because the fixed-income side was outperforming the equities holdings, the foundation was withdrawing its cash (for operations and grants) from the equity side, exacerbating the imbalance even more. That was good for the foundation in the short term, but Conte well realizes that the imbalance just as easily could have hurt the organization.

Conte emphasizes the need for deciding on the financial goal that the reserves are trying to achieve and defining clear guidelines for investment managers to follow to prevent them from engaging in a *style drift,* or, starting out in one kind of investment but then gradually losing focus and drifting off into others. In that regard, Conte said that the group is not so much looking at re-evaluating its equity-fixed income ratio as it is examining what the fixed-income category's objective is. If it's invested too highly in corporate junk bonds, for example, its value would tend to track with the foundation's equity holdings, thus defeating the purpose of diversification.

Another change to the foundation's strategy will be to make sure it rebalances its portfolio on a regular basis. "We didn't do that under our previous manager's guidelines, but with Cambridge that is going to be a regular behavior," says Conte. The foundation is in the process of deciding just how often it will rebalance.

Board and staff on the same page

In addition to their each having investment road maps in place, another commonality shared by the organizations discussed in this article and sidebar is the involvement of both the staff and the board in creating and updating the strategies. APTA's Martin speaks of the board's willingness to allow the association to dip into its reserves once the rainy day hit. At PMMI (see article beginning on page 157), the staff and the institute's investment adviser report to the finance committee annually on the economic climate. Finally, NACUA's Parsons, whose association went through a yearlong process revising the association's strategy (it hadn't been revised in 12 years), stresses the importance of board involvement. "I think there needs to be broad participation by the entire board," he says. "In fact, we went through a questionnaire phase of our entire board before we developed the policy, asking what the purpose of our reserves really is and how risk tolerant they were. The input at the beginning was crucial so that everybody was comfortable with it in the end."

Reprinted from
ASSOCIATION
MANAGEMENT,
April 1999

Setting and Meeting Your Association's Reserve Goals

By John P. Langan, CPA

One of the most critical factors in providing for the financial health of an association is maintaining the appropriate level of reserves relative to the organization's current and future financial obligations. Balancing resources to meet current and future obligations while providing member value is at the heart of any meaningful discussion of reserves. This concept is as applicable to trade and professional associations and their members as it is to the federal government and Social Security recipients.

When an organization is unable to meet its financial obligations over the short, intermediate, or long term, there is a devastating impact on perceived member value, staff morale, reputation of programs and leaders, and, ultimately, the organization's ability to survive. The primary reason why many organizations are "under reserved" is a lack of common understanding and consensus among association leaders as to certain basic issues:

- **What constitutes reserves?** Market value of investments? Amount of working capital?

- **Why are reserves necessary?** Why not reduce dues? Why not increase programs?

- **What is the appropriate level of reserves?** Investments equal to six months of expenses? Net assets equal to 50 percent of total assets?

What constitutes reserves?

Reserves are the unrestricted net assets—unrestricted assets less unrestricted liabilities—of an organization as of a given date. Reserves are the accumulated net surpluses of the organization or the net amount the organization would expect to receive were it to sell all of its unrestricted assets and pay all of its unrestricted liabilities at a given point in time. However, because most assets and liabilities are stated at historical cost, and because associations operate on many different time horizons—seasonal, annual, five-year strategic plan—the components of an association's reserves must be analyzed, matched to the periods over which they will benefit the association, and managed to maximize their return.

Figure 1 (see p. 27) shows a typical association balance sheet organized to reveal the components of unrestricted net assets or reserves, the reason for their accumulation, and the typical time horizon over which each component will benefit the association. Figure 2 (see p. 28) presents a pie chart that graphically illustrates the data in Figure 1.

While many associations and their investment advisers use the terms *reserves* and *cash and investments* interchangeably, it is clear from Figure 1 that cash and investments are not the sole components of available reserves. Furthermore, it is critical to classify available reserves pursuant to the time horizons and purposes for which they have been accumulated. For example, to say that XYZ association's operating reserves equal $150,000—operating cash—overstates operating reserves by $110,000 (that is, $150,000 in operating cash compared to operating reserves of $40,000).

This understatement is because such a definition ignores accounts payable and accrued leave that the association has already committed itself to pay. Furthermore, defining long-term investments of $250,000 as *long-term reserves* ignores the association's net equity in property, equipment, and so forth and therefore understates long-term reserves by the $820,000 noted in Figures 1 and 2. This reveals another common misconception among association leaders. The purchase of a building is not a use of reserves.

Figure 1

XYZ Association Reserves Allocation Worksheet
December 31, 1998

Operating reserves	Amount	Percent of total	Percent of budget [c]	Purpose/cycle
Operating cash	$150,000			
Accounts receivable	300,000			
Accounts payable	(195,000)			
Accrued leave	(165,000)			
Deferred dues [a]	(50,000)			
Operating reserves	**$40,000**	3%	1%	Fund operations/annual
Short-term reserves				
Short-term investments	$100,000			
Short-term reserves	**$100,000**	8%	2%	Supplement operations/1–3 years/ nonrecurring expenditures
Long-term reserves				
Long-term investments	$250,000	21%	6%	"Rainy day"/10–15 years
Property and equipment	950,000			
Mortgage payable	(150,000)			
Net property and equipment [b]	$800,000	66%	18%	Internal financing/financial health/ 20–30 years
Other assets	$20,000	2%	—	
Long-term reserves	**$1,070,000**	89%	24%	
Total unrestricted net assets (reserves)	**$1,210,000**	100%	27%	

[a] Deferred dues are sometimes ignored in calculating operating reserves as these funds generally would not be returned to members if an association were liquidated.

[b] Net book value of property and equipment less mortgage payable assumed to approximate market value.

[c] Assumed annual operating budget of $4.5 million.

An asset purchase of any kind is an allocation of reserves much like an investment allocation such as shifting from short-term Treasury bills to common stocks. However, remember that changing the asset allocation of the association's reserves will most likely affect the liquidity, time horizon, and returns associated with the underlying assets.

Why are reserves necessary?

To properly serve their members, associations must focus their strategic plans over several time horizons. Over the current operating cycle it is necessary to pay for budgeted expenses while supplementing the cash-flow squeeze brought about by seasonal dues receipts and meetings income. Over

Figure 2

XYZ Association Reserves Allocation
December 31, 1998

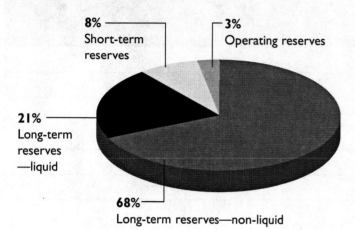

8%
Short-term
reserves

3%
Operating reserves

21%
Long-term
reserves
—liquid

68%
Long-term reserves—non-liquid

Long-term reserves—non-liquid	$820,000
Long-term reserves—liquid	250,000
Short-term reserves	100,000
Operating reserves	40,000
Total reserves	**$1,210,000**

the short and intermediate term, organizations must make one-time expenditures to launch new programs and provide for capital additions such as new accounting and membership systems. In the long-term, associations must ensure their ultimate existence by accumulating a source of internal financing available to temporarily cover a loss of core funding, a major restructuring, or some other significant event.

Accumulating reserves pursuant to each of these time horizons allows associations to match the programmatic needs defined in their strategic plans with the resources necessary to support them. Tracking and managing these reserves in a prudent manner demonstrates that a critical element of the board's fiduciary responsibility for sound financial management has been met.

What is the appropriate level of reserves?

Unrestricted net assets, and therefore reserves, grow by virtue of an annual positive change—through unrestricted revenues being greater than total expenses. Reserve ratios are most often expressed as a percentage of an association's operating expense budget. As noted in Figure 1, assuming a 1999 operating budget of $4.5 million, XYZ has total reserves of 27 percent— $1,210,000 divided by $4,500,000—or three months of budgeted operating expenses. *The ASAE Operating Ratio Report* (ORR), 10th Edition (1997) states that respondent associations defining reserves as total unrestricted net assets with operating budgets between $2 million and $5 million set a reserve goal of 46.2 percent or 5.5 months of budgeted operating expenses.

Using the ORR benchmark, XYZ is clearly under-reserved. Furthermore, only 11 percent of XYZ's reserves are allocated to operating and short-term net assets— $140,000 divided by $1,210,000—that represent less than one month's operating expenses (that is, $4.5 million divided by 12 months equals $375,000). Long-term liquid reserves represent 21 percent of total reserves, and 68 percent of reserves are allocated to long-term non-liquid assets. Therefore, in addition to being under-reserved, XYZ's allocation of its reserves is not properly matched with the needs of its annual operating budget. So what can and should be done? Consider the following real-world case study.

Establishing reserve goals— a case study

XYZ association received a management letter from its auditors containing observations and recommendations for improving its fiscal oversight. One such comment stated that the association's reserves had fallen from 50 percent to 27 percent of its annual operating budget over the past two years due to successive annual unrestricted deficits, meaning that total expenses were exceeding unrestricted revenue. These deficits resulted primarily from unbudgeted depreciation related to a recent expansion of facilities as well as from unbudgeted pension and other retirement expenses. Furthermore, the association's operating and short-term reserves represented less than one month's budgeted expenses, causing bank overdrafts and the need to liquidate long-term investments in seasonal periods of cash-flow shortages. Recognizing the serious risk posed by this situation on the association's financial health and the confidence level of its members, the XYZ finance committee took immediate action to remedy the situation.

The first step in this process was to review the prior-year budget against the audited results to identify and analyze the significant variances from budget responsible for the prior year's unrestricted deficits. This analysis revealed that the two items noted by the auditors were in fact to blame: namely, unbudgeted depreciation on assets purchased in conjunction with facilities expansion, and unbudgeted pension and other retirement benefits.

While the association had typically not budgeted depreciation and treated the actuarially determined cost of pension and retirement benefits "below the line," the committee quickly agreed that such items were an integral part of the ongoing cost of operations and therefore should be part of the association's operating budget. Accordingly, before approving the 1999 operating budget, the committee instructed management to provide for these items in the budget and to find offsetting revenue increases or expense reductions, or both.

The committee further instructed management to analyze the association's annual cash flow to determine the necessary level of operating and short-term reserves to avoid cash-flow problems, overdraft charges, and drawing on long-terms reserves to meet current and short-term needs. After reviewing these analyses, the committee adopted a budget and reserve policy that would provide for an operating budget—before long-term investment income—with a surplus equal to 3 percent of the association's expense budget. This annual surplus will be funded evenly between the association's short- and long-term investments to increase both short- and long-term reserves liquidity. Further, the committee agreed to propose a 2 percent membership dues increase in order for budgeted revenue to cover the full cost of operations and provide for the budgeted surpluses necessary to build reserves.

Finally, the committee agreed to recommend to the board that all investment income—both realized and unrealized—earned on long-term investments be credited to the association's long-term reserves and segregated for reporting purposes from the change in unrestricted net assets from operations. The return on long-term investments was budgeted at a conservative rate of 10 percent, consistent with the advice of XYZ's investment consultant based on the association's asset allocation, risk tolerance, and time horizon for these funds.

The board adopted the overall reserve strategy with the ultimate goal of providing for greater liquidity and creating over a six-year period a long-term reserve equal to 46 percent of budgeted annual expenses, as called for in the *ASAE Operating Ratio Report*. In conjunction with documenting and approving this policy, the finance committee and board instructed management to prepare a projection (see Figure 3, p. 30) that would clearly illustrate this reserve goal. This analysis will be updated by management based on actual results and periodically reviewed by the finance committee and board with further action taken as necessary.

Figure 3

XYZ Association Reserves Worksheet
FY 1999–2004

	1999	2000	2001	2002	2003	2004
Unrestricted net assets—beginning	$1,210,000	$1,370,000	$1,543,300	$1,731,149	$1934,918	$2,156,115
Change in net assets before long-term investment income [a]	135,000	139,050	143,222	147,518	151,944	156,502
Non-cash item—depreciation [b]	32,000	32,000	32,000	32,000	32,000	32,000
Addition to short-term investments [c]	99,500	101,525	103,611	105,759	107,972	110,251
Short-term investments	199,500	301,025	404,636	510,395	618,367	728,618
Long-term investment income—realized [d]	25,000	34,250	44,628	56,251	69,252	83,775
Long-term investment income—unrealized [d]	—	—	—	—	—	—
Total long-term investment income	25,000	34,250	44,628	56,251	69,252	83,775
Addition to long-term investments [d]	92,500	103,775	116,238	130,010	145,224	162,026
Long-term investments	342,500	446,275	562,513	692,524	837,748	999,774
Unrestricted net assets—ending [e]	1,370,000	1,543,300	1,731,149	1,934,918	2,156,115	2,396,391
Operating expenses—budget [f]	$4,500,000	$4,635,000	$4,774,050	$4,917,272	$5,064,790	$5,216,733
Unrestricted net assets as a percent of budgeted operating expenses	30%	33%	36%	39%	43%	46%
Short-term investments as a percent of unrestricted net assets	15%	20%	23%	26%	29%	30%
Long-term investments as a percent of unrestricted net assets	25%	29%	32%	36%	39%	42%

[a] Change in unrestricted net assets before long-term investment income budgeted at 3% of the annual expense budget.

[b] Depreciation assumed straight-line over 30 years.

[c] The addition to short-term investments is 50% of change in unrestricted net assets before long-term investment income and 100% depreciation. Interest earned on cash and short-term investments is included in the budgeted change in unrestricted net assets before long-term investment income.

[d] Long-term investment income budgeted at 10% annual return plus reinvested earnings and 50% of change in unrestricted net assets before long-term investment income. Unrealized gains and losses not budgeted.

[e] Unrestricted net assets—ending equals the sum of: unrestricted net assets—beginning; change in net assets before long-term investment income; and long-term investment income.

[f] Operating expenses budgeted at $4.5 million for 1999 projected to increase 3% per year.

How much is too much?

An association's ultimate reserve goals and strategies are not determined in a vacuum based solely on the projected financial health of the organization as benchmarked against its peers. As with all significant association decisions, setting and meeting reserve goals requires fiscal discipline as well as consensus among volunteer leaders.

In an association world in which boards turn over frequently and perception is often reality, association leaders must continually work to ensure that reserves are justified based on current and planned operations, and that this is effectively communicated and embraced by association stakeholders. One way association boards often justify reserves is by "designating" unrestricted net assets in financial statements to earmark reserves for specific purposes—operations, building, programs, and the like.

Unlike the for-profit world, where the Internal Revenue Service requires corporate taxpayers to justify or be taxed on "accumulated earnings," the IRS generally has not challenged not-for-profit organizations based on their level of reserves. The appropriateness of reserves has been viewed as a function of ensuring financial health while meeting the needs of members.

Some members have the perception that any operating surpluses should be used to reduce dues, increase services, or both. This having been said, experts have generally recommended that when total reserves exceed two years of budgeted operating expenses, an association should seek IRS approval for such an accumulation.

Setting and meeting your association's reserve goals requires fiscal discipline, a clear and well-communicated plan, and a consensus among association stakeholders and their advisers. Achieving these goals will help ensure the current and future financial health and viability of your organization while meeting critical member needs.

Staffing Issues

Restructuring Health Care Plans for Affordability

By Kathie Feldpausch, CPA

Reprinted from
Dollars & Cents,
ASAE newsletter,
November 2001

The only thing not difficult to understand about health care rates is the double-digit increases many employers have faced across the past three years as a result of increased health care spending—a point made at the Future 2001 presentation at the ASAE Annual Meeting and Exposition in Philadelphia.

Colin C. Rorrie, Jr., CAE, executive director of the American College of Emergency Physicians, Irving, Texas, and chairman of ASAE's Board of Directors, opened the session with this statement: "Health care expenditures are rising again, and neither managed care nor the government seems able to slow down the rise in health [care] spending."

Health insurance premium costs are particularly crucial at our association, the Michigan Association of Realtors, because salaries, payroll taxes, and benefits represent nearly 45 percent of our 2002 budget.

In addition, we face added competition in our employment market from state government and automotive employers that offer generous benefit packages. To stay within budget and retain employees, we looked at ways to reduce the costs of offering our staff a competitive health care package without sacrificing the benefits they perceive as valuable.

Cost-saving alternatives

Fortunately, as with many human resources management topics, educational assistance is available. Most insurance companies, faced with disgruntled consumers, have begun offering seminars, as have many professional organizations. I attended a workshop, "Reducing Costs in Your Employer-Provided Health Care Plans," offered by the Michigan Association of Certified Public Accountants (MACPA),

and our state chamber of commerce is offering an annual meeting session on containing health care costs.

Attending these sessions gives me valuable background materials for presenting financial alternatives to our CEO, finance committee, and staff. The Finance & Administration Section e-mail list has also provided me with ideas. Recent listserver discussions prompted me to run the numbers on passing a portion of the health care premium onto our employees. Although the numbers are favorable, the pretax employee cost amounts to nearly 2.5 percent of the average compensation of our nonsenior employees. Because we have budgeted to increase salaries by 4 percent in 2002 and have low participation in our Section 125 plan, this is not a reasonable cost-saving alternative for 2002.

Instead, we will begin with other measures, such as offering taxable cash compensation to employees who opt out of health insurance benefits. Tony Paschke, CPA, Consolidated Financial Corporation, Bingham Farms, Michigan, an MACPA seminar speaker, suggests an amount between $800 and $1,800, with no link to an insurance premium amount. We proposed a two-tier plan for our employees.

- $1,600 for a full opt out, with written proof of alternative coverage, or
- $1,100 for selecting individual versus family coverage (obviously for employees with eligible family members).

Structural changes

We found that we could save additional money by adjusting our plan structure. We met with our insurance account executive with the sole purpose of exploring alternatives that would allow us to keep our health insurance expenses in 2002 within 4 percent of the actual 2001 expenditures (our plan has fewer than 100 participants, so experience rating and negotiating directly do not apply).

We began by assessing our demographics. While our account executive cannot provide individual prescription or plan activity, she can provide counts—the average number of prescriptions per participant or the total number of hospital visits, for instance. Using these statistics, we can meet our budgeted goals by adding an in-patient deductible, increasing prescription co-pays, and adding self-insurance for a portion of the differential increases.

For example, the plan currently offers 100 percent in-patient coverage with no deductible. By adding a $500 per-family deductible, we will reduce the annual insurance premium by about 9 percent, or approximately $650 per employee. We will then reimburse an eligible employee for the deductible. Based on our employee demographics and historical data, we estimate five annual in-patient reimbursements at $500 each, or $2,500. The net savings to the association is $12,000. Once a written policy is created, employees must submit valid receipts for reimbursements.

We will incorporate a similar self-insurance plan for the prescription co-pay increases, and later this year, we hope to offer a financial incentive to employees who use the more cost-effective mail-order prescription service recommended by our insurance carrier.

Staff buy-in

We realized that we could not successfully make these changes without greater employee understanding on the issues, so we launched an in-house educational campaign. Shortly after the budget was approved, our human resources department sent a detailed e-mail to all employees outlining their benefits and related costs as approved in the annual budget. In addition, we are designing a brief employee benefits survey to test options and rate current services and programs.

In the future, employees will assume more responsibility for their health care spending, and health insurance benefits will require greater managerial oversight and proactive leadership. Working together, I envision that we can successfully identify shared-cost programs that maximize our available health care dollars and create long-term solutions.

Seventy-Five Ideas to Develop and Retain Staff (Parts I through IV)

By M. Suzanne Berry, CAE, and Valerie Brown, CAE

Reprinted from *AMC Connection,* ASAE newsletter, December 2000 –September 2001

Professional recognition/building benchstrength

1. Make sure that staff members feel as though they have significant control over their jobs and the ability to grow in their positions by taking on new responsibilities.

2. I hold administrative staff meetings every other week so that the unique perspective of [this group] is given a voice. In the normal press of business, these staff members are often the last to be consulted, yet they are the people who must get the work product out the door, so to speak, so their insight into which processes are working and which aren't are very important.

3. Once a month we hold a meeting in which a program officer or other department head gives a presentation so that administrative staff has a chance to better understand the work of the organization as a whole.

4. Recognition must be sincere, and employees can't be recognized for simply meeting expectations. That becomes a disincentive to those who strive for excellence.

5. We called in a personal development counselor to start off a more structured training program. We looked at time management, presentation techniques, and so forth, but also analyzed team members' personal and business goals. This exercise stimulated our push toward offering remote working options.

Personal recognition

6. Each birthday is celebrated with a lunch chosen by the celebrant, and staff takes turns making dessert.

7. We celebrate birthdays and anniversaries once a month with bagels. Prior to a person's birthday, staff circulates a card and everyone signs it.

8. We recognize birthdays with a cake or dessert of the celebrant's choice. The staff gathers in the kitchen and we share the dessert. This is a brief get-together and is a fun break in the afternoon.

9. We have a monthly gathering to celebrate any personal event a staff member wants mentioned; for example, birthday, anniversary, birth of child or grandchild. After the food and social part, the gathering becomes a staff information meeting.

10. We instituted a 10-Year Anniversary Club. An elegant dinner is planned for new and returning inductees and includes spouses or significant others. An impressive plaque is presented during the dinner. Staff display these with pride and clients always make a note of them during tours.

11. We redesignated everyone as team members rather than members of staff.

12. In December, we take a late lunch and don't come back. We take the staff to a nice restaurant and enjoy ourselves. The president passes out holiday bonus cash, says a few words, and we leave when we want.

13. During December we take the entire staff and a guest each of their choice to a nice dinner. The president and his wife usually give theme gifts to the staff. For example, we went to a Chinese restaurant and we all received a nice wok and gift set.

14. We have staff luncheons several times during the year. The office is closed during this extended lunch and everyone attends. These are especially nice rewards for the staff when we have just finished a particularly busy month. They are not staff meetings; we just enjoy each other's company and share some laughs.

15. One of the most well-received things I did was to have a surprise ice cream social. I brought in fun flavors of ice cream, nuts, candies, and so forth, and gathered everyone in the kitchen. The staff appreciated it and talked about it for a long time afterward.

16. Having staff work toward goals that have an immediate reward, such as a gift certificate to a department store or a certificate for free time off, has been successful for me. I've been careful not to make the incentive part of a competition among team members, however. The criteria for rewards need to be based on the individual's performance, not on how he or she performs compared to other employees.

    For example, I wanted my staff to learn the answers to questions they were constantly asking me. I gave them a study guide and set up a test day. The reward was based on the score received: $75 gift certificate for 95 or higher; $50 for 90–95, and so forth. They learned a great deal, which helped me, and they had a nice reward.

Flexible work schedule/time off

17. We often provide extra days off, depending on workflow. The Friday after Thanksgiving, the third of July (this year), and an extra day or two around the holidays are very welcome.

18. As equally appealing as the flexible work schedule is extending sick leave to cover time off for immediate family members in an employee's routine care. The willingness of an organization to accommodate individual circumstances is highly valued and makes for happier employees.

19. Be flexible with temporary scheduling issues so that staff members can spend time with their new addition, deal with a child care crisis, or go back to school.

20. The most popular thing we introduced was the compressed work schedule. It's really improved staff morale.

21. In addition to the national holidays, each staff person gets his or her birthday off. He or she may select when to take it—it needn't be the exact day.

22. Many of my staff members are parents, and they know they can take time off to go to the doctor, school, or a game and not be penalized. They know what needs to be done and we don't look over their shoulders or make them punch time clocks. No one has ever taken advantage of this.

23. We instituted a reduced workload schedule a few years ago to accommodate staff members who needed to reduce their hours. Staff receive benefits depending on the level of hours, including earned time.

24. My partner and I have traditionally closed the office between Christmas and New Year's Day, giving the staff an extra week of paid vacation. Often each of us comes in to work during that time, but it is by choice. Our clients have no problem with it.

25. We have an earned time policy that combines sick and vacation days. There is a graduated scale that increases the longer a staff person is with the company. We start out at 10 hours a month for full-time staff and

a prorated amount for part-time staff (more than 25 hours a week). Staff manage their earned time and the record keeping is much simpler. Honesty also is upheld, as staff do not need to use a sick day for a vacation day.

26. We recently had an employee start working from her home after the birth of her baby. She had been with the company for more than 11 years, and we didn't want to lose her. She had a computer at home, and we allowed her to take one printer. She has access to her files, e-mail, and voice mail. She comes into the office once a week, on a set day and time, for meetings with staff members and to gather work and mail.

27. We recently instituted a flexible work schedule. Employees work eight hours per day, between 7 a.m. and 6 p.m., with core working hours being 10 a.m. to 4 p.m. This new policy has allowed staff to have more flexibility in scheduling doctor's appointments, spending time with family, and so forth.

28. We instituted casual dress during the summer and close the office two hours early on Fridays in August.

29. A flexible work schedule is one of the most important benefits to offer in today's work climate.

30. Recognizing that employees have a personal life and allowing flexible scheduling make them feel valued.

31. Put into place policies for compressed time and telecommuting programs.

Benefits

32. We recently upgraded our benefits to help us hold on to our staff in this competitive market.

33. Before changing health insurance companies and benefits, the entire staff discusses it. While they're not given a wide range of choices, their input is valuable in the final decision.

34. We became aware of long-term care insurance and found that the cost of providing it for ourselves was equal to the cost of offering a basic plan to all our staff, allowing them the option to upgrade. Even our younger staff appreciated this option. The ultimate cost to the company for seven policies was no more than we would have paid for the two of us. Several of our staff chose to upgrade their plans at their cost.

35. We have a laptop complete with Internet, e-mail, and the software programs that the staff use for conferences, board meetings, and so forth. However, the staff also are allowed to use the laptop for personal use when it is not needed for business. This is of benefit to staff members who do not have home computers. We do this with a reservation system, and of course, business use takes precedence over personal use.

36. We care about the health of our team members, so we not only offer private health coverage for those who want it, but as a small gesture we provide free fruit in the office.

37. We provide movie passes to each staff member and a guest. The passes are good at any theater in the country, so some staff use them when traveling.

38. We have a program whereby each employee (there are 10 of us, including clerical and mailroom staff) has a personal development budget that is used in consultation with his or her supervisor. This is for "training and development that is directly related to our business and to your position." People use this to join associations; go to seminars, meetings, and conventions; order study programs; and so forth.

What I have learned across time is to structure our program so that it is a cost-sharing deal. The company will reimburse the individual half of his or her expense up to the limit of the budget. Previously, the company paid the whole amount, and I found that sometimes people might join some type of local association and never participate or attend a meeting. Or they might go to a meeting or convention without having considered the value of the expenditure of money and time. This way, they give much more thought before joining, buying, or going. We also get much better reports on what they learned, which we share with everyone.

39. Our company contributes 50 cents on the dollar up to 6 percent of an employee's salary. They are vested after one year.

Motivation

40. A periodic assessment is distributed to all staff. The surveys then are sent anonymously to a third party to tabulate. The results are shared with staff and become the basis for updating the company's strategic plan.

41. Involve staff in determining resource issues and needs as well as in the decision-making process. This creates ownership of the decision.

42. Walk-around management is important to understand workloads and to see how problems are being resolved. You also can assess how people are interacting.

43. We always have made it clear that we will help anyone move on or move up. We have always provided continuing education and served as a reference.

44. Once a year we take our staff on a retreat. We pay for the hotel rooms, meals, mileage, and so forth. We close the office on a Friday and spend that day in a meeting room with flip charts, reviewing our work processes and discussing how we can make our services to our clients more efficient and cost-effective. We review our clients' strategic plans and major goals. On Friday night, we treat everyone (including spouses, guests,

and kids) to dinner. On Saturday, we take it easy together. We then pay for everyone to stay over Saturday night with no planned activities. Interestingly, most come together to do something as a group Saturday night. Since opening our doors in 1984, this retreat exercise has created some lasting bonds among staff members.

45. Sometimes we rent a houseboat and take the staff out on that for a day. The houseboat approach is not as productive as a hotel, as we have only one day together, and it's hard to get into the work mood on the boat. But it does have a real bonding effect.

46. Via our accountants, we asked staff to give us their evaluation of the company (its strengths, weaknesses, etc.) and then used this feedback to come up with an overall score of how we are doing. This told us a lot, as there were big differences in scoring. This helped us in our business development strategy.

47. While we can't stay on the cutting edge of technology, we do try to regularly upgrade and purchase computer equipment and software. If something comes out that will benefit the staff and how they do their work, or perhaps ease some frustration with the current equipment or software, we try to get it as soon as possible. I believe this helps motivate staff or at least helps them to not become frustrated with old or obsolete tools.

48. We found that there were often communication breakdowns. So now, every last Friday of the month, we hold a one-hour team meeting where everyone presents a brief report on his or her main projects and ideas. Each team member takes his or her turn to moderate these meetings, and we follow up the sessions with a team lunch.

49. It's not always possible to set aside time for structured training and

exchange of best practices. Recently, the team members agreed that they would be happy to come into the office on occasional evenings for training sessions (when the phones are not ringing and client demands can be put on the back burner). We will set up the first one soon—probably on techniques for researching on the Internet—and provide participants with some hospitality in return for their time.

50. We were always very secretive about our financial performance but we are now sharing more financial information with the team.

51. The key words are *communication* and *participation* when it comes to keeping team members motivated. Of course, this is easier said than done. As with any small company, it's difficult to keep a balance between serving the immediate demands of the clients and nurturing your human resources and development of the business.

52. We have a "good news" notice board so that we can share compliments from clients and other successes.

53. We provide candy and other snacks in the office. This erases the need to run downstairs for a snack to satisfy the afternoon munchies.

54. We have a staff happy hour. About once every three months, we get together in our conference room or kitchen and discuss the company's successes and goals over light food.

55. In past summers we have had a pool party at the boss's house during a weekday afternoon. The office closed at lunch, and we went home to get our spouses and children before going to the party. Mexican food was catered by a local restaurant. These events lasted as long as anyone wanted to stay (usually early evening) and the kids had a blast. It has formed some lasting friendships and great memories.

56. What really makes a difference for staff retention and development is to make sure that the staff members feel as if they have significant control over their jobs and the ability to grow in their positions by taking on new responsibilities.

57. I try to establish a good, solid working relationship with my team by taking them to lunch occasionally to talk about something besides work.

58. We redecorated our offices, which excited and motivated staff considerably.

59. Hosting a quarterly *good-news* lunch, which is a communication and sharing session. It is used to introduce new staff, pay out employee recruiting bonuses, share AMC news, and talk about clients and client transitions.

60. We encourage open communication by not having walls in our offices.

Compensation

61. We have just instituted and budgeted a bonus system. Staff who have demonstrated added revenue, reduced expenses, and *above-and-beyond* effort are recognized.

62. Our performance-review process is tied to goals that are mutually agreed upon by the staff person and his or her supervisor. Meeting and exceeding expectations are also discussed so the staff person knows what is expected in order to achieve the highest rating.

63. We provide comp time in return for days worked on-site at meetings. The comp days are to be taken within 30 days of returning to the office.

64. Three words: holiday bonus cash.

65. We encourage team members to maintain three ongoing goals for the coming six months and to evaluate progress on these. Goal setting and achievement then form part of their assessment for bonuses.

66. We abolished our (traditional) Christmas and mid-year bonuses as they had lost meaning in terms of representing rewards for good work. We now have a bonus pool from which I can make payments as achievements are made. There have been some winners and losers in this process, but no one has complained.

67. When a new staff person is brought into the company, the successful employee-recruiter receives $400.

68. We keep track of overtime and comp time worked by exempt staff leading up to a major meeting or event. Bonuses are given based on the time contributed by each employee. This helps keep staff motivated during those long preparation weekends.

Recruiting

69. Use temporary agencies when additional staff support is needed. This gives you a chance to assess perform-ance—and screen potential new employees.

70. We pay a recruiting fee to staff members who recommend candidates for employment.

71. We place newspaper advertisements soliciting new employees. Internet-based employment sites—such as Monster.com—are also a great resource.

72. Networking in association and business circles is a great way to recruit new employees.

73. Use an agency to run employee testing and background checks.

74. The entire staff interviews prospective candidates, and each staff member is given an equal vote.

75. Prospective employees are taken through at least three interviews, regardless of the level of the available position.

Best Strategies for Employee Motivation

By Stacia H. Bontempo

Reprinted from
Executive IdeaLink,
ASAE newsletter,
July 2001

Faced with tight budgets, association executives often consider implementing casual dress days, employee picnics, and extra comp days to jump-start employee motivation. While helpful, a successful employee-motivation strategy requires broader consideration from association CEOs.

Marshall Colt, managing principal, Corporate Psychological Management, LLC, Denver, reports that simply "giving employees *something* is the basic mistake in employee motivation." The true motivator, according to Colt, is a leadership style that is respected and adheres to ethical behavior. "When employees perceive their leader is unselfishly working for the good of the organization and they are confident in the path the organization is taking, they will work even under the most arduous of conditions."

If the staff feel that their leader has only salary in mind when making strategic decisions, they may feel that he or she does not have a clear vision for the organization. "Vision is a key element," says Roxanne Emmerich, author and speaker on organizational change and president, The Emmerich Group, Minneapolis. "Most organizations have a mission statement but not a true vision." Employees need a clear vision of what success looks like. Emmerich's example: Bill Gates told his employees that he wanted a computer on every desk in America. He did not tell them how to do it, which could stifle creativity. He simply shared his vision and allowed his employees to "think outside the box."

A leader also needs to have an excellent understanding of organizational culture. According to Michael A. Knaus, principal, Michael A. Knaus & Associates, an organizational performance consulting firm in Rochester, New York, "Executives need to be less isolated and insulated. They need to see and understand what the *front line* is going through to really boost productivity and morale." If leaders make all their decisions in a vacuum, then they are not allowing their staff to help create a direction for the organization and thus to feel like contributors to the organization.

While a negative culture, a poor salary or incentive plan, criticism, toleration of poor performance, and limited resources all contribute to low morale, the lack of guidance and mentoring from managers is truly damaging. Emmerich points out that "employees quickly lose their desire to do extraordinary things because of many of the things that managers do that they learned in business colleges. People don't want to be commanded and controlled. They want to be unleashed. Most of what we learned in school about how to manage does more harm than good."

It's simple to implement a blanket approach to motivational strategies when managing employees, but experts say it doesn't work. A leader can provide pizzas on Fridays as a motivational tool, but that may only temporarily motivate those who aren't dieting. And some employees might like public recognition for a job well done while others may not. Listening carefully to what individual employees need is essential, because each responds to different motivators.

Knaus suggests implementing monthly performance dialogs in addition to the traditional annual review. "This is an excellent opportunity to listen, to give guidance and praise, and keep an employee focused." Sometimes motivation can be as simple as a little appreciation shown at the right time. A monthly dialog provides the perfect framework.

Knaus also recommends conducting an exit interview when staff leave, especially when an organization suffers from high turnover and low morale. He reports that more than 50 percent of staff who resign may be leaving not because of money, but because of other reasons, such as not being challenged or mentored by their managers.

Once you've bolstered your leadership style and feel confident that you truly understand what employees need and want, you can elect to round out your motivational strategy with feel-good tactics such as on-site massage, paid maternity leave, and exercise club memberships. It is a good practice to ask employees to implement these programs. If you find that most employees feel that dressing casual is important, ask a group of employees to draw up a plan and take responsibility for its implementation. "This will give them a sense of control in the organization and invest the responsibility of a program's success or failure on the employees," says Colt.

Knaus says, "Some younger employees in their 20s and 30s may not be looking at their job as a long-term commitment, but a place to gain some experience. That's particularly true if they are just starting careers, making career changes, or do not see any long-term advancement plan that they can follow within the organization." If a manager or leader were to make them more accountable in their positions and create a career ladder for them, they would be less apt to jump. Training is another tool that often keeps staff motivated, Emmerich added.

The notions of good leadership and careful listening to employee needs remain essential to motivating as well as retaining employees. Colt suggests that leaders "remember their beginnings, because every leader was once an employee."

Top 15 Affordable Staff Incentives

By Kim Stoneking, CAE

Reprinted from

ASSOCIATION

MANAGEMENT,

July 2002

If you share my experience as a leader of a small-staff association, you no doubt would like to find creative ways to reward your staff. As one who has taken my staff for granted far too often and has not customarily offered perks and incentives, admittedly I struggled somewhat to come up with a good number of original ideas for this article. Through the ASAE listserver I have an entire network of peers I can contact when needing input and ideas on any topic. They contributed to the ideas that follow.

The List

Clearly, when I do make that conscious effort to reward my staff, I sense an almost immediate improvement in spirit and morale. Employees of associations with small staffs often wear many hats and work tirelessly on various projects and assignments. Small rewards and incentives that express appreciation make for a satisfied staff and help with retention. Consider using some of these staff incentives.

1. Allow staff to purchase old computer equipment. You may even consider giving it away.
2. Give a staff member the use of complimentary hotel accommodations for a getaway weekend following a big event or for a special anniversary.
3. Offer special days off aside from regular holidays and vacation time: birthday, anniversary, a holiday shopping day, a mental health day, and so on.
4. Celebrate special days (employment anniversaries, start of a new fiscal year, end of a major event) with chocolates, a gift certificate, or the employee's favorite coffee or dessert.
5. Close the office for an afternoon, on a slow day for the staff to take in a movie or go bowling.
6. Ask your association members for help. They often have access to vacation homes, tickets to special events, the theater, or professional sporting events. I know of association members who have kindly provided a beach house, a ski chalet, a retreat site in the mountains, and even an unused time-share.
7. Provide a gift certificate for a massage, or arrange for chair massages in the office during hectic times.
8. Return from your travels with a small gift for each employee.
9. Give a relax bag containing a video rental coupon, microwave popcorn, theater candy, and a couple of sodas.
10. Permit a half-day off a month for staff to work with their favorite charities. (Some follow-up may be necessary.)
11. Reward employees with a gift certificate to a favorite bookstore.
12. Provide a coupon or ticket for a carriage ride. Most metropolitan areas offer them.
13. Bring in homemade goodies on a regular basis.
14. Give a holiday wreath or centerpiece. It's a gift that lasts, and the staff will think of you and the association often.
15. Put a special thank you to a staff member in your association publication.

Paying for it

For the most part, I've tried to include ideas that are inexpensive or even free. Still, some of these items do cost something. If you have a personal expense account provided by the association, make room for these types of expenses during the budgeting and planning process. Tell your board or finance committee what you are planning to do. Knowing what it means to the staff, they should be supportive. Finally, for even more ideas, check out *1001 Ways To Reward Employees* by Bob Nelson and Kenneth H. Blanchard (1994, Workman Publishing Co.). Remember, as the cliché goes, it's the thought that counts—so be creative.

Special Report: Conducting Legal Employee Evaluations and Performance Appraisals

By Maurice Baskin

Reprinted from
Association Law & Policy,
ASAE newsletter,
February 1, 2002

Today's economic uncertainty has forced many association executives to at least consider reducing staff size in order to salvage the fiscal health of their organizations. While these staff cuts are sometimes true *reductions in force* based not on the performance of the affected individuals but rather on a decision to eliminate or outsource certain departments, association executives will often look to cut staff whose performance levels are below expectations.

Of course, the decision to terminate an employee for cause should be made only after the association has taken great care to ensure that it is not exposing itself to significant legal risks. When calculating these risks, an employee's past performance evaluations—documented in writing—can serve as the association's best ally or its worst enemy, depending on how effective and accurate those evaluations are.

Conducting proper employee evaluations is not only important for associations looking to minimize their risks when defending employment decisions that are attacked in *abusive* or *wrongful* discharge cases, equal employment opportunity (EEO) charges, or arbitrations. When properly planned and conducted, employee performance evaluations and appraisals can also be an important tool for increasing employee morale, motivation, and productivity.

On the other hand, improper employee evaluations can actually be used against an employer and can subject the employer to an increased likelihood of litigation. In addition, the employee evaluation process may be subject to the federal Uniform Guidelines on Employee Selection Procedures, 29 CFR Part 1607 [specifically Sections 2(B) and

(C), and Sections 4(C), (D), and (E)].

The following guidelines will help associations develop and implement employee performance appraisal systems that meet practical and legal criteria:

1. **Develop an appraisal form that relates specifically, or can be adapted to relate specifically, to the employee's job.**

   The most important step in the development of a good performance appraisal form is the development of an accurate and detailed job analysis or, at least, a good job description. The performance appraisal should then be directly related to the employee's job description or detailed job analysis, which should be *incorporated by reference.* In the best situation, the performance appraisal should detail and rate each aspect of the employee's job analysis.

   The evaluation should also distinguish between major and minor components of the job. For example, if your job evaluation uses a *point* rating, the employee should be able to earn more points for good performance in the major aspects of his job, and fewer points should be allocated for those aspects of the job requiring a minor degree of the employee's ability, skills, education, or time.

2. **Train the evaluators.**

   An employer may have a top-notch appraisal form, but that form is not worth much if the individuals using it are not properly trained. Evaluators should be given written instruction on the purpose and mechanics of the performance appraisal system, emphasizing the importance of accuracy and including information on the potential EEO problems and directions on relating the performance appraisal to the job analysis or job description. Associations should update these instructions and require evaluators to review them before each series of evaluations. It is important to document that this has been done by, for example, requiring some signed statement from the evaluator that he has reviewed the instructions.

Supplement written instructions with group training in order to answer evaluators' common questions and concerns and to help lessen the disparity among evaluators.

3. **Develop a rating scale.**

The employee should be appraised in terms of how well she behaves in performing each job duty and how well her performance reflects a particular job-related trait. Typically, the evaluator will rate the employee's behavior somewhere between *unacceptable* and *exceptional*. It is preferable, however, to develop ratings that are more descriptive, better tailored to the job, and allow the evaluator to describe how he arrived at his conclusion.

Thus, with regard to a general trait such as *resourcefulness*, the choices available to the rater might range from *unable to solve problems unless given specific guidance* to *frequently develops creative and original solutions to unexpected and unusual problems*, with two or three degrees in between.

4. **Safeguard against inaccuracy.**

The most typical problems affecting the accuracy and reliability of evaluations include evaluators being too easy on employees, giving *middle-of-the-road* rankings, or forming a general impression and assigning that rating to all performance aspects,

without distinguishing an employee's strong points from weak points.

One safeguard against inaccuracy involves the evaluator providing *relative rankings,* in which employees are ranked against one another, from best to worst in terms of job performance, or by placing an equal number of employees into one of several performance levels. This approach is particularly useful when wage increases are based upon appraisal scores. Such relative rankings, however, are based on the assumption that employee performance will conform to a normal distribution curve.

Another common system involves the evaluator ranking or comparing an employee's performance against what is expected, not against the performance of other employees. Obviously, unless highly developed, this system is subject to the rater's tendency to *go easy* on employees or score them all at the same level. Accuracy can be improved if appraisals are tied to specific job-related criteria or lists of job duties and job-related traits.

5. **Ensure against bias of the evaluator.**

Associations must emphasize the EEO aspects of employee evaluations in training evaluators and should caution evaluators against stereotyping employees. Employers should monitor the evaluations performed by each evaluator to determine if there are actions or language in performance evaluations that reflect bias or stereotyping.

6. **Provide for crosschecks on evaluators.**

An appraisal system's reliability is generally enhanced if two or more individuals separately review employees or if the initial reviewer's evaluation is reviewed by another evaluator. All evaluators should have personal knowledge of the job duties and performance of employees being rated.

7. **Get the employee's agreement.**

An employee's agreement that the job duties on which he has been rated are accurate and complete can prevent later debates. If the employee disagrees with the evaluator's statement of his duties, he should be required to explain how and why.

8. **Upon review, require employees to sign their evaluations.**

The employee should be required to sign his evaluation, even if he disagrees with the evaluator's assessment of his performance, and care should be taken to ensure that the employee's signature is dated. This will help to establish the beginning of a statute of limitations for filing complaints relating to the evaluation and will also undermine the employee's attempt to attack an evaluation with which he previously agreed.

9. **Provide for appeals on grievances.**

Allowing the employee to appeal his appraisal to a higher-level supervisor enhances the employee's perception of the evaluation process as fair and promotes good employee relations, as long as the appeal process is legitimate. Failure to exercise this right of appeal may be damaging to the case of any employee who later wages an EEO or wrongful discharge claim.

10. **Establish a schedule for evaluations.**

It is often advisable to more frequently evaluate new employees and employees who are on probation. And remember that inconsistency in the scheduling of evaluations can, like any other inconsistency in employment actions, become the basis for an

EEO charge or undermine the employer's reliance on evaluations in its defense of EEO or wrongful discharge cases or arbitrations.

11. **Review performance evaluations for adverse impact.**

When performance appraisals are used as the basis for decisions such as promotions, transfers, and discharges, the evaluations are subject to the federal Uniform Guidelines on Employee Selection Procedures. If the selection process negatively affects protected minorities or females, each component of the selection process, including the performance appraisal, must be independently evaluated for adverse impact.

If it is determined that the performance appraisal has caused an adverse impact, the employer must demonstrate its job relatedness. If the appraisal cannot be validated, the adverse impact must be eliminated through changes in the evaluation or the procedures by which it is implemented.

12. **Follow the established system.**

Courts are increasingly finding that employers have made binding contractual commitments to their employees. Evaluators should be careful to follow all previously stated procedures and avoid making commitments to their employees that cannot be fulfilled.

Editor's note: The guidelines contained in this article are not intended as legal advice or opinion. Such advice can only be given following consultation and discussion of particular facts and circumstances.

Reprinted from
Dollars & Cents,
ASAE newsletter,
December 2001

Saying Goodbye: Employee Terminations

By Michael Hoagland

Saying goodbye is difficult—for those leaving and those staying behind. But by treating your departing employees as well as you treat your new employees and saying goodbye with dignity, compassion, and concern, you'll be saying as much about your organizational culture as you will about how you welcome newcomers. It also makes the transition easier for those left behind if they know former colleagues are treated fairly and compassionately.

Develop a plan

When your organization determines it must cut expenses, including staff positions, it is best to develop a process beforehand that management agrees on and to which all decision makers can adhere. Difficult staffing decisions will have to be made, and a predetermined plan will help management stay the course.

1. **Determine members' needs and analyze organizational priorities.** Use a strategic plan or member survey. If neither is available, develop a quick feedback mechanism for your board of directors or governing body. Although each organization needs to develop its own process for cutting costs and reducing staff size, all associations should craft a plan that ensures legal compliance and fairness and obtains the best results.

2. **Determine the core competencies needed to fulfill your mission.** Only after the needs assessment is complete and the core competencies are analyzed can staffing issues be addressed.

3. **Analyze the talents within your organization, and match them with the core competencies.** If specific job responsibilities are on the hit list, then discuss which staff members will be affected. Can an existing employee, whose current responsibilities are not at the top of the new priority list, cover other more important issues for the organization? Many associations have talented, adaptable staff, and a well-managed organization will use existing talent to cover any shortfalls in the new organizational scheme.

In addition to determining the future needs of your organization and deciding which staff will leave the association, you also should consider any legal questions that might arise. During the process, an association must keep in mind questions regarding:

- the Age Discrimination in Employment Act of 1967,
- race,
- gender,
- compliance to the employee handbook and employee contractual agreements, and
- the Worker Adjustment Retraining Notification Act.

The involvement of human resources staff is invaluable throughout the process because they will:

- be familiar with the association's policies and procedures;
- know applicable local, state, and federal laws;
- identify additional talents employees may have to help the restructured organization;
- prepare the necessary paperwork;
- train management for termination discussions; and
- assist in the exit process.

Notifying staff

Once the staffing analysis is complete, management should inform those affected as quickly as possible. Conduct termination discussions with staff in one day. Nothing hurts staff morale and organizational credibility more than employees hearing through the grapevine that their positions have been eliminated.

Have a plan, arrange times, and prepare scripts for supervisors. In addition, have all necessary paperwork prepared for departing staff. This exit paperwork should contain information on:

- severance and vacation pay,
- medical coverage,
- outplacement services, and
- retirement and unemployment benefits.

If staff have their own offices, it may be best to go to them. That way, employees are in their space and can close the door once you've gone. The bottom line is maintaining respect, care, and concern. Be sure to offer transitional support—encourage staff to call the human resources department or come to you with any questions.

Maintaining morale

After all employees have been notified, gather the remaining staff. Tell them why the staff reduction was necessary, let them know that it is over, and acknowledge the contributions of the departing staff. It is important to be honest and transparent in order to maintain credibility and focus the team on the future. Create an environment that allows staff to ask hard questions, and share your vision for the future with them.

Most likely, more will be asked of everyone. If you can, adjust salaries immediately for staff who will take on the greatest amount of responsibility.

Using outside resources

Look to the following resources if your organization is considering downsizing:

- American Society of Association Executives,
- Society for Human Resource Management,
- outplacement firms, and
- consultants.

When faced with downsizing, it is important to develop an equitable process, keep staff informed, take care of departing employees, support the remaining staff, and focus on the future.

Reprinted from
Dollars & Cents,
ASAE newsletter,
January 2000

Contingent Employees: Do the Benefits Outweigh the Disadvantages?

By Maureen R. Smith

Managers and top-level executives often find that implementing a downsizing plan in their organization is about as pleasant as wrestling an alligator. For this reason, many are turning to contingent or contract workers to supplement their staff. Contingent workers offer the benefit of flexibility without long-term commitments. Employers know that if business lags or times get tough, they can sever the relationship without the fuss or guilt normally associated with downsizing. Using contingent workers gives an organization the ability to react quickly and efficiently when conditions change.

In a recent survey conducted by Business and Legal Reports, more than 90 percent of the 1,110 respondents said that contingent workers were part of their staffing mix, a 50 percent increase from five years ago. Almost 60 percent indicated that they expected to use increasing numbers of contingent employees across the next five years. In 1997, the Bureau of Labor Statistics (BLS) estimated that 12.5 million workers out of a total workforce of 126.7 million had what it calls "alternative work arrangements." Of the alternative workers:

- 8.5 million were independent contractors;
- 2 million were on-call workers;
- 1.3 million were employed by temporary staffing services; and
- 800,000 were employed by contract firms.

The number of workers hired by temporary and leasing agencies has expanded most rapidly, doubling in the past 10 years and quintupling since 1982, according to BLS

findings. According to the 1997 survey "Beyond Downsizing: Staffing and Workforce Management for the Millennium," by Lee Hecht Harrison, there are many advantages to using contingent workers:

- flexibility;
- lower benefit costs;
- instant staff;
- lower overall staffing costs;
- rapid availability of workers;
- no severance costs;
- prescreening; and
- access to additional skills.

Of course, such advantages don't come without a price. The survey noted the following disadvantages of using contingent workers:

- possible lack of job commitment;
- possible lack of organization-specific skills;
- high turnover;
- lower morale;
- difficult to integrate into core staff;
- higher salary costs; and
- possible compromise of organization's security.

How good are they?

Some employers are concerned that contingent workers are less competent and less committed to their work than permanent employees. But according to a recent Pace University study, contingent workers may be just as motivated as permanent employees. New findings of the attitudes, behaviors, and motivations of contingent workers shatter many myths about this sector of the labor force. "Far from being less committed, less satisfied, and less skillful than core employees, contingent workers frequently scored higher in such areas of this survey," said Peter Allan, a professor of management at Pace University's Lubin School of Business in New York. "Management should not overlook the potential of these workers. Despite their lack of job security and other benefits, contingent workers certainly have the motivation to function productively." Organizations need to tailor work to motivate contingent workers and give them direct feedback on their performance to maximize motivation and production, Allan said.

Allan surveyed 197 professional and technical workers, both core and contingent, about how they perceived their jobs. Then he assessed those attributes that are linked to motivation and performance, such as task significance, autonomy, skill variety, and feedback. The study shows the following:

- Contingent workers scored higher in their ability to be self-motivated by their jobs. One possible reason: Because they lack permanent positions, contingents may value their jobs more, while permanent workers may take their jobs for granted.

- Contingent workers scored significantly higher in task identity and job feedback. One possible reason: They are hired for tasks that are whole, identifiable pieces of work and that provide information about the effectiveness of their performance.

- Contingent workers scored higher in need for growth, suggesting that they were likely to respond more favorably to jobs that challenged them.

With the exception of job security, the core workers did not score significantly higher in any category, including in their satisfaction with compensation. In many cases, professional and technical contingent workers are paid better than full-time employees are. "Generally, contingent workers do not enjoy the same kinds of benefits that full-time employees do, such as pensions or health insurance," Allan said. "But in many cases, people choose to be contingent workers because it allows them job flexibility. Often hired for a special project, they leave when the assignment is complete, thus freeing them to care for an aging parent or young children. This type of temporary work also can be ideal for a retired person who wants to keep a hand in the labor force."

Who's who?

Not sure who your contingent employees are? Experts disagree on how to define and count contingent workers. They are given many labels: temporaries, contract firm workers, independent contractors, and on-call workers. BLS assigns definitions to each:

- Contingent workers are those who have no explicit or implicit contract and expect their jobs to last no more than a year.

- Temporary help agency workers are paid by a temporary help or staffing company.

- Contract firm workers are employed by a company that provides them or their services under contract or leases, are usually assigned to only one customer, and work at the customer's site.

- Independent contractors are consultants, freelance workers, or contractors, who can be either self-employed or wage and salary workers.

- On-call workers report to work only when called.

Here are some general guidelines for determining the status of your workers. Workers are more likely to be employees, not independent contractors, if they

- work on your organization's premises, not at home or their own work space;

- have been employed by you for a long time;

- work only for your organization;

- work with your tools and equipment; and

- follow a schedule that you set.

In addition to the issue of defining contingent workers, remember to consider the worker classification for tax filing purposes. Check with your CPA for more information.

The Art Of Outsourcing

By Andrew S. Lang, CPA

Reprinted from

ASSOCIATION

MANAGEMENT,

February 2000

The Tire Association of North America (TANA) has four regular meetings, a major annual meeting, and no meeting staff. TANA has a bimonthly magazine, a biweekly newsletter, and a weekly news service on its Web site—but no publication staff. It has significant government relations activity, but no government relations staff. And, despite intensive use of technology, information systems staff are nowhere to be found.

If you want to confirm any of these details, don't ask the receptionist. She or he, as well as all the support services, plus all the furniture and equipment, except the laptops, comes with the offices that TANA rents in Reston, Virginia.

Dave Poisson, CAE, who engineered the change from the traditionally operated but overstaffed and money-losing operation he inherited to this model of outsourcing, says that the association was nearly out of business when he was hired as executive vice president with a $2.6 million budget and 3,800 members. Now the association, which has a $3.5 million budget and 5,700 members, is thriving. Membership is growing, and a strong bottom line is allowing Poisson not only to rebuild reserves but also to invest in new programs. No wonder Poisson is referred to as "the father of the virtual association."

I chose to begin this article with the TANA example because, while it may seem extreme, it indeed reflects the outsourcing trend we're seeing in every dimension of association management. In these challenging economic times, where rapid change is constant and functional solutions essential, no broad-ranging solution is more strongly embraced by associations than outsourcing. So ubiquitous is outsourcing that I felt it was time to do some research on the topic before offering advice about its successful deployment.

You'll read in the following pages what we know about outsourcing in large and small associations as demonstrated through a recent ASSOCIATION MANAGEMENT survey, my review of outsourcing literature, and insights from association executives. The picture that emerges from these sources is that, at a minimum, outsourcing has the possibility of giving your organization a competitive advantage. Outsourcing at its best enables you to excel at your core competencies while your outsourcing partners excel on your behalf in their core competencies.

Changing the way we do business

Why the interest in and use of outsourcing? The answer may be found in the various pressures weighing heavily on today's associations. To begin with, there is the matter of economics. Associations are under pressure to provide additional services or employ expensive new technologies—often in circumstances when resources (e.g., dues income) are harder to come by and competitors are becoming more aggressive.

Solutions for associations facing this dilemma—short of mergers, alliances, and bankruptcy—include raising revenue or cutting costs. Raising revenue is time consuming and can be initially costly both financially (for instance when new programs are being developed) and politically (for instance, when an association tries to raise dues significantly).

This leaves cutting costs as the more likely alternative. One option—to terminate programs that have lost their viability—is often quite challenging politically because even smaller, older programs invariably have a vocal constituency. Another alternative is outsourcing.

The growth of outsourcing. In years past, associations have contracted with vendors to handle a variety of activities—usually cyclical or specialized (e.g., payroll preparation)—that for one reason or another the organization itself preferred not to undertake.

The National Association of Women in Construction, Fort Worth, Texas, which has 6,200 members and six full-time employees, has outsourced the convention director position for four years. "Our outsourcer usually comes in one day a week, depending on the workload, but otherwise she works from home," explains Dede Hughes, executive vice president. "We contract annually for her services, but her workload varies widely. As we get closer to the convention we take up more and more of her time. Not only do we save on space and equipment, but we also don't have to provide benefits. It works well for us, and she seems quite pleased with the arrangement as well."

The current labor market. The second substantial pressure facing associations is the current labor market. Simply put, no matter what job an organization is trying to fill, filling it will be a challenge. Based on conversations with association executives, many turn to outsourcing because of the difficulty in finding and keeping qualified people.

If a function is outsourced properly, the association can be reasonably certain the task will be accomplished. For certain activities, the risk associated with having the work done wrong by marginally qualified staff can outweigh even a potentially higher cost for outsourcing the job.

The labor shortage has also created the problem of too many senior association executives performing basic tasks that divert their attention from more important responsibilities. This can result in diminished quality of essential services and products. With key staff being stretched thin doing today's tasks, far too little thought is being given to the association's strategic issues.

Highlights of the ASAE survey

To investigate the extent of outsourcing in the association industry, I prepared a survey that ASSOCIATION MANAGEMENT sent to 3,600 association chief executive officers nationwide. More than 650 responses were received, of which 621 had sufficient data to be useful. The survey listed 34 activities that could be outsourced and 13 possible reasons for outsourcing. In addition, it requested respondents to identify themselves by type of entity (e.g., 501(c)(3), 501(c)(6), or other) as well as by size of staff. For purposes of the survey, *outsourcing* was defined as "contracting with a vendor to provide a recurring internal activity."

Almost all respondents indicated they outsourced a variety of activities. Only 21 of the 621 responses indicated the association was outsourcing only one activity or none at all. The average for all respondents was 7 outsourced functions, and more than 20 percent indicated they outsourced 10 or more activities.

These figures might be viewed with circumspection given that those who outsource were more likely to respond to the survey than those who did not. Nevertheless, information provided in responses was quite interesting.

For instance, by far the single most popular activity to outsource was legal services, as noted by 442 of the 621 associations responding. Given that 44 percent of the respondents have 1–10 staff and a total of 73 percent have 50 staff or fewer, outsourcing legal services to this extent makes sense; associations that size generally do not need and cannot afford a full-time general counsel.

It is not surprising that payroll services, given its particular nature, was second in popularity, being outsourced by 61 percent of the associations responding. Pension administration, another complex technical task, was third at 54 percent. Web design and development was outsourced by 52 percent, and thus was a close number four in popularity. This result indicates the pervasiveness of the need for the service, as well as the apparent challenge many smaller associations feel in taking it on. (See Table 1, p. 57, for a complete list of activities outsourced according to the ASSOCIATION MANAGEMENT survey.)

Table 1

Activities Currently Outsourced

Activity	Total Count	Percent*
Legal services	442	71
Financial services—payroll	377	61
Pension administration	337	54
Web site—design/development	323	52
Financial services—investments	257	41
Web site—maintenance	234	37
Business travel arrangements	232	37
Tax compliance	219	35
Financial services—accounting	198	32
Benefits administration	175	28
Maintenance of association's building	167	27
Information systems/technology	156	25
Advertising	150	24
Surveys–member needs/market research	146	24
Government relations	131	21
Publications	128	21
Financial services—lockbox/cash receipts	108	17
Public relations	86	14
Staff training	85	14
Mailroom activities	81	13
Recruiting—temporaries/regular	79	13
Strategic planning/implementation	78	13
Meeting planning/management	61	10
Fulfillment	59	10
Telecommunications	45	7
Data management	38	6
Marketing	27	4
Sales—telemarketing	26	4
Development/fund-raising	23	4
Sales—direct mail	21	3
Product development	13	2
Membership development	7	1
Customer service center	4	1
Sales—Other	4	1

ASSOCIATION MANAGEMENT'S outsourcing survey, October 1999.

* Percent is total count divided by total valid responses received.

There was not a great deal of difference between what 501(c)(3) and 501(c)(6) organizations are outsourcing. However, there was an enormous difference in the relative number of respondents. Of those identifying themselves as one type or the other, more than twice as many respondents indicated they were 501(c)(6) trade associations. The survey was sent to a representative sample of ASAE's membership, of which 501(c)(6)s make up 45 percent and 501(c)(3)s make up 44 percent—illustrating that outsourcing is by far more popular with associations whose members are businesses.

Corporate comparisons

It appears that the nonprofit world is only beginning to catch up with the for-profit world. The U.S. market for outsourcing was $100 billion in 1996 and $164 billion in 1998, according to The Outsourcing Institute, a New York City-based organization that keeps tabs on outsourcing in the world of larger for-profit organizations.

The New Corporate Cultures, by Terrence E. Deal and Allan A. Kennedy (Perseus Books, 1999), offers additional fascinating insights. For example, in the mid-1990s Nike (which continues to be the leading global supplier of athletic shoes) operated with "fully 100 percent of its shoes. . . produced by contract manufacturers."

Outsourcing obviously has "bottom-line" appeal for corporations, as several books and studies that explore both the short- and long-term thinking behind such arrangements indicate. However, few such studies have been done on outsourcing in the nonprofit world, and certainly none with so great a sample of the association world in particular. Thus the results of the ASSOCIATION MANAGEMENT survey should be of particular value to the association industry.

Rationale for outsourcing

If you're contemplating outsourcing, you'll probably start your investigation by learning why your fellow executives have done so and to what extent they've been sat-

isfied with the results. Table 2 (see p. 59) provides the results of the survey's inquiries regarding reasons for outsourcing. Each respondent was allowed three selections out of 13 options. The primary reason for outsourcing, by a wide margin at 61 percent, was to "gain access to expertise," followed by "focus on core activities" at 44 percent, and "lower operating costs" at 38 percent.

Practically speaking, these results might be interpreted to say, "There are many skills that we know we can get better expert assistance with from the outside. In addition, we'd rather focus our efforts on more essential activities. Besides, we're pretty sure we can save money."

The top three results matched the top three results of The Outsourcing Institute's most recent *Annual Survey of Outsourcing End Users* except that the order of priority was reversed: First and foremost large for-profit institutions outsourced to "reduce and control operating costs;" "improving company focus" was second; and "gain access to world-class capabilities" was third.

Like the good for-profits they are, corporations want to save money and keep their focus on what is most important. But even they, big as they are, acknowledge that it is simply not possible to bring all the specialized expertise needed by a business in-house. Outsourcing becomes a solution to ensure focus on core activities.

The Outsourcing Institute's Web site www.outsourcing.com offers a current perspective on core competencies based on a conversation between Frank Casale, president of the New York City-based institute, and Maurice F. Greaver, president of Greaver and Associates, Centreville, Virginia. Greaver is the author of a recent, excellent text on outsourcing and teaches strategic outsourcing for the American Management Association, New York City.

"Core competencies are the innovative combinations of knowledge, special skills, proprietary technologies, information, and/or unique operating methods that are well integrated into the processes that provide the product/service benefits that cus-

Table 2

Reasons for Outsourcing

Activity	Percent*
Gain access to expertise	61
Focus on core activities	44
Lower operating costs	38
Better manage the activity	31
Improve service to members	27
Enhance association's flexibility	17
Improve products	15
Acquire new ideas	13
Lower investment in assets	9
Reduce association's risk	5
Enhance competitiveness	5
Change fixed cost to variable	5
Increase revenue per employee	0

ASSOCIATION MANAGEMENT's outsourcing survey, October 1999.

*Percent is total count divided by total valid responses received.

tomers value and want to buy," says Greaver. "Core competencies are what create the attributes that make the organization's products/services different, and more importantly, what makes the customer want to buy the products/services. Organizations compete for customers, revenue, market share, [and so forth], with products/services that meet customers' needs. Accordingly, without core competencies, organizations cannot compete."

For example, a specialized medical association might be able to provide information about cutting-edge breakthroughs that is unavailable elsewhere; members may share

information not yet available to the public. While this access is itself a core competency, when combined with the ability to organize and run educational events members need and want—and can get nowhere else—you have the clear differentiation that identifies a true core competency.

Care obviously must be taken not to outsource core competencies. To do so essentially strips the organization of its competitive ability. But what else can go wrong with outsourcing? Just about everything.

Outsourcing pitfalls

Every management technique has its successes and failures, and outsourcing is no exception. In *Insider Strategies for Outsourcing Information Systems* (Oxford University Press, 1999), authors Kathy M. Ripin and Leonard R. Sayles mention a variety of generic problems generally relevant to outsourcing, such as companies whose sales pitch is considerably better than their product and the fact that many outsourcers want to fit your problem into their solution.

Fortunately, the vast majority of ASAE survey respondents were extremely satisfied with their outsourcing experience. The overall level of satisfaction expressed by respondents was 83.5 percent. Some areas such as payroll services and tax compliance ran as high as 94 percent. The lowest level of satisfaction was represented by "sales-other" at 65 percent.

Nevertheless, the responses indicated that the association world has its share of outsourcing failures as well. Beverlee Lee, chief financial officer of the American Legislative Exchange Council (ALEC), Washington, D.C., provides a prime example. ALEC employed a national conference coordinating firm to provide registration and housing for its annual conference. "Things went sour from the very beginning," says Lee. "This conference provides critical cash flow for us. Since they were doing the registration, they input the financial activity into their system. However, they never provided us with timely reports as to what had been received. As a result, I had serious cash-flow concerns.

I had to wait until the bank statements arrived to determine where we stood. They just didn't seem to care."

ALEC had another, more serious problem. "Instead of having a 24-hour or 36-hour turnaround in confirming registrations, the company was taking two weeks," recounts Lee. "As a result, we were inundated by member calls."

While ALEC initially believed the outsourcing organization was large enough to handle the conference, it became clear that it was insufficiently staffed. Lee believes that a more thorough review of references might have helped. In any case, "…as a result of the problems, the association has decided to bring the work back in-house."

Thomas J. Dammrich, CAE, president of IPC-Association Connecting Electronics Industries, Northbrook, Illinois, reports a similar "capacity" problem at the heart of a failed outsourcing relationship. A fulfillment center's sales pitch stated in a forthright manner that it would be able to handle the 600–800 orders a month the association currently handled. However, after the first month, the fulfillment center's system overloaded, and its monthly reporting system failed entirely. As a result, regular reports promised to the association were not produced.

A multitude of complaints from members about the fulfillment center resulted in extra work for association staff and led to the demise of the outsourcing relationship within a year. "This was the old over-promise and under-deliver," notes Dammrich, who says he's unsure as to what more he might have done—"perhaps spending a day on site or getting additional references would have helped and perhaps not."

For more insight into why services are brought back in-house after an outsourcing agreement has been entered into, it is worthwhile to study the results of two surveys included in Mike Johnson's book, *Outsourcing in Brief* (Butterworth-Heinemann, 1997). The International Facility Management Association (IFMA), Houston, conducted these studies in 1993

Table 3

Disadvantages of Outsourcing

Response	Percent*
Contract employees less Company oriented	51
Lengthy bid process	44
Longer response time to problems	35
Loss of control	31
Poor-quality workers	29
Difficult to change vendors	25
Reduced quality	24
Time consuming to supervise contracts	23
Low level of service	23
Increased turnover	22
Increased costs	18
Burden on purchasing	12
No disadvantages	9

Outsourcing, International Facility Management Association, 1993 (used with permission).

* Percent reflects number of respondents noting particular disadvantage divided by total number of respondents.

on the subject of outsourcing "facilities management" (on-site information systems management). While the results are most relevant to technology management, they represent typical outsourcing problems.

The first survey identifies a dozen disadvantages of outsourcing. (See Table 3.) The problems did not reflect ills of a catastrophic nature, but rather the kind of things that would make this type of relationship less desirable. For example, the number one problem was a lack of dedication on the part of contract employees—something one might expect, especially in an endeavor

Table 4

Why Outsourced Services Were Returned In-House

Response	Percent*
To better control quality	66
To reduce costs	54
To regain control	50
To improve quality	50
To improve response time	45
Dissatisfaction with provider	35
No longer needed	12
To reduce turnover and training costs	7
Service no longer available	2

Outsourcing, International Facility Management Association, 1993 (used with permission).

* Percent reflects number of respondents selecting a particular reason for bringing an outsourced service in-house divided by total number of respondents.

where emergencies and long hours can be the norm.

IFMA's second survey (see Table 4) tells the greater tale of woe. The survey is based on situations where management of on-site information systems was outsourced but brought back in-house when the relationship failed. These reasons for failure have a nightmarish quality, given that two of the top three focus on loss of control, and the second (suffered by more than half) indicates escalating costs.

Furthermore, these surveys do not reflect a host of related problems: managerial time lost, difficulty in finding the right type of staff to do the job in-house, and other negative impacts on the organization of a failed outsourcing relationship. Both surveys do emphasize the absolute need to move quite carefully in setting up an outsourcing arrangement the right way, with the right people, the first time.

Establishing outsourcing relationships beneficial to all parties takes more than wishful thinking. In both my review of the literature and my discussions with association executives, certain advice about how to achieve success kept recurring.

Routine monitoring. First, ongoing project review must be conducted by an association staffer who is both a good communicator and who is familiar with the project or service being provided. This monitoring, which needs to occur weekly or even daily at the beginning of the relationship and regularly thereafter, should include not only such issues as cost, timeliness, and quality, but also the overall success of the relationship, including the reduction of pressure on the association.

Prompt action. Should problems arise, deal with them promptly. Your contract should anticipate "counterproductive" relationships and provide escape clauses.

In other cases, problems will arise because the organization changed, the context changed, or the world changed, and adjustments need to be made through no fault of the outsourcer. Anticipating that changes will take place can reduce conflict and create opportunities to facilitate ease of operation and good teamwork.

Deciding what to outsource

With a good perspective on how best to go about outsourcing, the next question is what to outsource. Identifying which activities should be outsourced and when is not an exact science. However, by giving weight to the various reasons why associations in general have outsourced, it is possible to develop a sense as to both the propriety of outsourcing a specific task and the best order for outsourcing a series of activities.

The "Outsourcing Evaluation Tool" (see sidebar, p. 65) was developed for just such a purpose. To use this tool, one assesses a value from 0 (problematic to outsource) to 10 (great potential benefit from outsourcing). Any result approaching a score of 100 indicates outsourcing should at least be considered. A result of 100–140 (the maximum) indicates that outsourcing would likely be quite beneficial.

Each of the variables, described here briefly, was referred to consistently in conversations with association executives and in survey responses as reasons an association decided to outsource various functions.

Core/non-core. Outsourcing a core activity is potentially quite dangerous—most would say unthinkable. Assume, for example, that a small association in a highly specialized legal niche decided to outsource content development for its annual conference. Even though it is possible that the association could find a technically proficient outsourcer, the chances of that provider being sufficiently astute about both the technical, cutting-edge issues in the field and the intricacies of the politics of the association are small indeed.

If an activity is determined to be a core competency, forget the tool. If the score is not a "0" or "1" for this variable, rate it and continue.

Instability/stability. Every business needs to avoid instability. Not only is it a problem in and of itself, but it creates other problems such as loss of staff. While outsourcing can cause instability at its inception because of new procedures and new reporting relationships as well as changes to its in-house staffing, it can help solve previously existing problems.

Higher operating costs/lower operating costs. Any change that will reduce cost without otherwise endangering operations will generally be positive. If you predict higher operating costs due to outsourcing, first determine if you have taken into account all the costs of undertaking the operation in-house. The next step would be to review the need for additional bids. If costs appear to clearly favor doing the work in-house, seriously contemplate doing so because acting otherwise will likely raise questions on the part of leadership. Nevertheless, if other factors point strongly toward outsourcing, higher cost should not, in and of itself, be a dissuading factor.

Inefficiencies/increased efficiency. While

this issue is often considered simply a matter of cost savings, the truth is that inefficient operations also have a negative impact on staff: They know when they are performing redundant, inefficient tasks, which is demoralizing. A true advantage of outsourcing is that the activities being outsourced will be looked at by an independent party that specializes in the activity and should be able to develop efficiencies, if not immediately, within the first year of operations.

Less flexible/more flexible. The question here is a crucial one: Will the association become more flexible in its ability to deal with its environment and core activities by outsourcing this function? Any managerial change that will make the association more nimble will make it better able to compete and to excel.

High risk/lower risk. Outsourcing a function may reduce the risk an association faces, or it may not. To outsource payroll is likely to reduce risk, since the job will be taken over by experts who, in addition to greater expertise, may well have additional liability coverage. Alternatively, outsourcing an activity when the association's staff has built up important institutional knowledge certainly incurs risk should either the original outsourcer fail or the outsourcer and key staff turn over in an untimely fashion.

Reduce member satisfaction/increase member satisfaction. If outsourcing a function will increase members' satisfaction and the relationship seems reliable, it would appear to be a good decision.

Stagnant ideas/new ideas. One benefit of employing great outsourcers is the likelihood that they will have new ideas to enhance association operations or product lines. It is a rare association staff that can regularly come up with good, new, "outside the box" thinking while undertaking their regular tasks.

Fixed costs/variable costs. Most in-house operations are considered to be fixed because it would generally take layoffs to reduce them. Outsourcing agreements often are fixed as well, but can be set up to vary based on the level of activity.

Easy to maintain/difficult to maintain. Finding the right individuals to staff a particular activity and keeping those individuals has proved to be one of the most rigorous challenges that many association executives face. In addition, managing certain activities is simply more challenging than managing others.

Basic skills/cutting-edge skills. Associations must accept that if all tasks are to be done exceedingly well, they cannot all be done in-house. Practically speaking, the use of new technologies is often limited by the capabilities of those who operate them. Thus, it is rational to consider looking to outside organizations that are able to provide individuals with continually upgraded, cutting-edge skills.

Inability to grow/ability to grow. Many associations are limited in their ability to take on more activities because current staff is spread too thin. Outsourcing certain activities frees more experienced staff to engage in new tasks. In addition, some associations are simply short on space, so outsourcing creates more room for core activities.

Small capital requirements/large capital requirements. Any activity that requires minimal investment can more easily be kept in-house. Such things as costly technology upgrades require investment plus expensive staff training. Keeping capital available for new programs and reserves is a clear benefit to the association.

Difficult to outsource/easy to outsource. Always take the ease or difficulty in outsourcing a function into consideration. Not only will there be a challenge in dealing with reasonably concerned staff, but the learning curve requires a substantial investment of time both by staff and outsourcers. Most associations will also find themselves initially having to "sell" the concept to their board and officers.

New mind-set emerges

In discussing outsourcing with members or with senior staff, don't focus simply on the near- and long-term future of the association, but also on how outsourcing will be used in the future. One change that is occurring in the for-profit world is a reconceptualization, from outsourcing a task to outsourcing responsibility for results. Many term this "business process outsourcing."

Using technology as an example, what in effect is being said is, "We need to have our information flow assured. This is an area changing so fast that we will not try to stipulate how you will do it, we will simply agree on the desired outcomes. How you reach those outcomes on an ongoing basis is your responsibility."

Something else I'm seeing in the for-profit world is the creation of the role of director of outsourcing. If this level of focus is being placed on outsourcing, can nonprofits afford to ignore it?

Consider this observation from *Strategic Outsourcing* regarding corporate America's current perspective on outsourcing: "Historically, outsourcing was used when organizations could not perform, perhaps due to incompetence, lack of capacity, financial pressures, or technological failure. Now outsourcing is being used to restructure organizations that have been quite successful. These organizations now recognize that management's undivided attention on building core competencies and serving customer needs is critical. Anything that distracts from this focus will be considered for outsourcing."

Keep in mind, however, that outsourcing is not right in all situations and for all time. Gail G. Kincaide, CAE, executive director of the Association of Women's Health, Obstetric and Neonatal Nurses (AWHONN), Washington, D.C., sheds light on this reality. AWHONN had outsourced the exhibit management portion of its annual convention for decades when it became clear that it was time for a change.

"Strengthening our relationships with our industry partners had become a new thrust in our strategic plan. This made us rethink the situation," explains Kincaide. "We found that our volume of this type of activity had risen so that we were paying more outsourcing a part of a person's time than it would cost us to hire an exhibits manager. In addition, we really needed the perspective of a senior-level marketing expert in-house to promote AWHONN's convention and all other products and services in a unified fashion. Perhaps most importantly, having this new level of strategic thinking and expertise available full time for our senior staff and board was also essential."

What was not core had become core again; what had been well priced became expensive. Outsourcing, like so many other management techniques, can be of great value if used wisely, but it is not a panacea. A decision to outsource should be made when conditions indicate it is appropriate. However, given that circumstances change, it's critical to revisit outsourcing decisions from time to time and re-evaluate whether this particular solution is still the best one for your association.

Seeking a Desirable Outsourcer

1. Look for an outsourcer with substantial, relevant experience in the association industry.
2. Don't rely simply on a prestigious name as a guarantee of good performance.
3. Remember that experienced outsourcers know each new project will involve challenges.
4. Expect outsourcers to be flexible. Avoid "cookie cutter" solutions.
5. Meet with the specific staff at the outsourcing firm who will work on your job.
6. Make sure the outsourcer will always allow you to accept or reject staff.
7. Look for an outsourcer who is interested in meeting your staff.
8. Look for an outsourcer who will help develop your RFP, including providing ideas on the kinds of questions that ought to be asked.
9. Find out how the outsourcer keeps up with the latest technological and business advances.
10. Ask outsourcers how they ensure quality.
11. Look for an outsourcer who can explain how the organization has maintained successful working relationships on projects similar to yours.
12. Ask the outsourcer to describe new ideas provided to other associations.
13. Confirm that the goal of both organizations is to continuously improve whatever is the subject of the outsourcing agreement.

Outsourcing Evaluation Tool

Concerns	Rating (0–10)**
1. Core/Non-core	
2. Instability/Stability	
3. Higher operating cost/ Lower operating costs	
4. Inefficiencies/Increased efficiency	
5. Less flexible/More flexible	
6. High risk/Lower risk	
7. Reduce member satisfaction/ Increase member satisfaction	
8. Stagnant ideas/New ideas	
9. Fixed costs/Variable costs	
10. Easy to maintain/Difficult to maintain	
11. Basic skills/Cutting-edge skills	
12. Inability to grow/Ability to grow	
13. Small capital requirements/ Large capital requirements	
14. Difficult to outsource/Easy to outsource	

*The reason not to outsource is listed first, and the potential benefit of outsourcing is listed second.

**Where 0=problematic to outsource, and 10=great potential benefit from outsourcing

Results:
- 70 and below   Do not outsource
- Approaching 100   Consider outsourcing
- 100+ and above   Outsourcing should be beneficial

Sealed With a Contract

Reprinted from

ASSOCIATION

MANAGEMENT,

February 2000

By Jeffrey P. Altman

As you finalize selection of an outsourcing partner and focus on specific terms and conditions of the deal, it's time to begin thinking about your contract. No matter how simple or complex the undertaking, and whether the contract is a few pages or a volume, it is critically important to set forth the key terms and conditions, clearly and in plain English, so that everyone knows what is expected.

This is also the best time (while the vendor is still trying to get your business) to address and resolve potentially contentious issues, which will help avoid later misunderstandings and disputes. In drafting your contract, keep these basic principles in mind.

- **Specify expected outcomes.** Describe the specific services the vendor has promised to perform in objective, quantitative terms. Provide a timetable for completion of tasks against which the vendor's performance can be measured.

- **Maximize your leverage by making payments in steps.** Don't pay the vendor everything at the outset. Instead, require progress payments linked to the successful accomplishment of mutually agreed-upon milestones. Retain the right to withhold further payments and to terminate the contract for cause, if the vendor fails to perform as promised.

- **Prevent unacceptable personnel changes.** Especially with service contracts, it is critical to specify the individual(s) who will work on your project. Make sure the association has the right to approve any personnel changes or to terminate the contract if the vendor tries to substitute someone who is unacceptable.

- **Get ownership of intellectual property and protect your confidential information.** Stipulate that the association owns all intellectual property and other work product developed at its expense. Request the vendor to agree to preserve the confidentiality of any association information and prohibit the vendor from using confidential information, such as the names and addresses of your members, for its own commercial purposes.

- **Include a changes clause and other standard contract provisions.** Require any changes in performance, schedule, or price to be approved in advance in writing by the association as well as pre-approval rights for any substantial out-of-pocket expenses. Include a disputes resolution clause that may provide for mediation/arbitration and requires any litigation to be brought in the jurisdiction most convenient for the association. Finally, ask your vendor to indemnify the association for any claims or damages resulting from the vendor's errors or omissions.

- **Include special provisions** that apply to the type of services (e.g., meeting management, computer software) being outsourced.

- **Be careful what you sign.** Not long ago, at the end of a feel-good meeting, an association initialed a vendor's proposal for certain services. The association believed it was just confirming that the vendor was hired for 1999, but the proposal described the services the vendor was willing to provide through 2003. You can guess what the vendor is now arguing. The lesson to be learned? The only preliminary document you should sign is a letter of intent that your lawyer has reviewed. It's rarely worth the effort, however, and you're usually better off just skipping the preliminaries and negotiating the contract itself.

- **Carefully review the vendor's contract form.** Even if the vendor insists on using its own contract form, have your lawyer review it and propose whatever changes and additions are necessary to preserve and protect your rights. If your vendor is unwilling to negotiate a fair and reasonable contract, beware of how it will treat the association once it has a signed contract. It may be time to revisit your vendor selection decision.

Reprinted from
ASSOCIATION
MANAGEMENT,
February 2002

Managing a Sparsely Staffed Editorial Operation

Editorial experts shared tips and resources for the small-staff publishing department at a roundtable discussion presented last fall by the Washington, D.C., chapter of the American Society of Business Publication Editors. The panel provided a number of actionable ideas for associations with limited budgetary and human resources to devote to their publications operation.

- **Establish solid vendor relationships.** "Respectful relationships with your vendors are critically important when producing your publications," said Kathleen Sheehan, editorial consultant and former editor-in-chief at International Technology Education Association, Reston, Virginia. Sheehan recommends making a true assessment of your own limitations so that you can find publishing professionals who can fill in the blanks.

Supriya Nayalkar, executive editor, *Communications Technology* (the journal of the Society of Cable Telecommunications Engineers, Exton, Pennsylvania), added that if one person or vendor is outside of your editorial loop, there can be a domino effect. Consequently, Nayalkar sets long deadlines to allow for unanticipated problems. Janine Orr, president, Orr Communications, Inc., Richmond, Virginia, also stressed the importance of teamwork, recommending to carefully choose the players who will be working on your publications and their produc-

tion. Particularly when choosing a printer, look for value-added services (preflight inspections, in-house mailing, postal approvals and processes, labeling, inserts, and so on), as well as exceptional customer service qualities.

- **Agree on goals and set a design direction.** Meredith Menkin, project manager, EEI Communications, Alexandria, Virginia, suggested providing overall guidelines for the working partnership as well as specific details for every project. Similarly, Orr advised to make a list of objectives for your publication. Meet with your staff (or perhaps volunteers) to determine what would and would not be visually appropriate for your publications—and your industry—in terms of image, color choices, and so on.

- **Institute practical efficiencies.** Menkin collects all information about a project in one place, updating as she goes, and keeping everyone informed of deadlines, content or design changes, and any other alterations. *Communications Technology's* Nayalkar admitted that members of her small work group wear a lot of hats, with crosstraining and collaboration being the norm. "We also have to learn new production skills and software programs to increase our speed and efficiency," she said. "Since we've learned to use Quark, editors can post things to the shared system and keep it moving."

Tips From a One-Person Publications Department

Reprinted from
ASSOCIATION
MANAGEMENT,
February 2002

Lisa Tocci, managing editor, *Lubes & Greases,* the award-winning monthly magazine for the lubricants industry, was the single staff person producing the magazine until about a year ago. While she used the occasional part-time person to assist with advertising sales or update the database, it was her solo situation that resulted in the development of a number of efficient practices that she continues using even though her staff is expanding. Here are a few of her time savers.

1. If possible, shift your workday to either 9–6 or 10–7. That way, you can switch off the phone at 5 p.m. and have two hours of quiet, productive time—and a lighter commute.

2. Discipline yourself to open your e-mail only three times each day. That way you won't be tempted to distract yourself by responding to the steady flow of communication.

3. Do not provide a chair for visitors. They'll spend less time in your office.

4. Look for royalty-free photographs and images. Three of Tocci's favorites: Photodisc.com, Images.com, and Digitalvision.com. If you need something else, consider buying images on disk; many contain hundreds of images for quite a small price.

5. Travel at least four times each year. It aids your creativity to be exposed to outside groups and affiliated organizations. Tocci follows the two-story rule: Every trip should generate two solid story leads.

6. Review your printer's contract at least every three years so your printing partner doesn't become complacent. There are emerging technologies all the time—and lower prices—so be sure that you know about them.

Finally, says Tocci, "Don't beat yourself up when things just don't go right. Muzzle your inner critic and move on."

Membership

Letter From the Chair: Membership Marketing in Turbulent Times

By Rick Whelan

Reprinted from *Membership Developments,* ASAE newsletter, July 2002

Recent events—the September 11, 2001, terrorist attacks, anthrax scares, downsizing and layoffs, and our sluggish economy—have made for a time that most membership professionals won't soon forget, although I'm trying.

Perhaps the only good thing to come out of the last several months is that we've all received a collective *kick in the pants* when it comes to membership recruitment, retention, and renewal efforts, which is a good thing from time to time.

For the past several months, I've come across many associations with troubled membership marketing programs, low recruitment, and dwindling renewals. Most often they've tried to right themselves by cutting back on marketing or pulling out of the market altogether, which, I consistently tell them, is a mistake.

Although associations may need to trim programs or address problems masked by the good times of the 1990s, cutting and cost containment only go so far. We've got to sell our way out of the downturn. We must market ourselves better, and we can, if we follow a common-sense approach. Let me share five observations.

First, to attract new members and keep the ones we have, we've got to get in front of them. Now is not the time to cut back on our overall marketing efforts. You are guaranteed two things when you stop marketing: lower numbers and less revenue. Fight the urge to concede your long-term membership goals for short-term savings.

Many of you know that I work for an agency that teams up with about 60 national nonprofit associations. Although several of them have had some downturns in their membership numbers, many have actually grown, and one is reporting that 2001 will be its best year ever in acquiring new paid members.

Your association can grow—or at least hold its ground—when you stick to the basics. Have a written marketing plan in place for growth, and don't be afraid to change it depending on market conditions. Know the mathematics of our profession, and you'll instinctively find the path to follow. Remember: It's always cheaper to keep them than to get them. If you have a limited budget, focus on renewals at the expense of acquisition.

Further, listen to the market and respond accordingly. Stick to the programs that work; drop the others. Don't be afraid to fail in trying to grow. One colleague told me he had been marketing *on his heels,* and now he had to get up on his toes.

Second, a recent publication cited a McGraw-Hill study that concluded, "Organizations that keep their marketing programs going during tough times actually recover faster than those who don't." Those associations cutting too far into their marketing efforts will likely be the last ones to recover, if they recover at all.

Third, now might be an ideal time to grow your market share. While rival organizations pull back on their marketing, you might have a unique opportunity to capture their members and customers.

Fourth, during economic hardship, accountants look for ways to trim costs, and their memberships in your association are prime targets. Can members see the value and benefits they get from their dues? They should. Right now, a member needs your association for networking, industry information, job leads, and selling opportunities. You must define your benefits to match people's needs and wants.

And fifth, tough economic times don't last, tough membership professionals do. Plan as if the economy will get better. It will, I promise.

CEO to CEO: What Proactive Steps Are You Taking to Retain Members in the Current Economic Climate?

Reprinted from
ASSOCIATION
MANAGEMENT,
February 2002

We have made a conscious decision not to pull back, not to take a "wait and see" stance with regard to retaining members. We are moving directly into a major marketing initiative to rebrand the association. The idea is to develop messages and images that more clearly express our identity and the value we create for members and prospective members. We are getting better at marketing to our mission. And we know from past experience that this will positively affect retention.

We're also moving forward with planned investments in our infrastructure by piloting several programs this winter designed to strengthen chapters, where the majority of our members make contact with us. We are delivering six "taking it to the states" orientations facilitated by trained volunteer leaders. State officers are relieved of the burden of programming activities, we open up new avenues of opportunity for volunteer leaders, and we raise the bar on training and accountability. All of this enhances value at the local chapter level and that means better retention.

Gary Krysler, *Executive Vice President, Women's Council of Realtors, Chicago*

The question of retaining members has a whole new meaning following the September 11, 2001, attacks. We are primarily an individual membership organization and we've been reaching out to our members in a number of ways (conference calls, virtual forums, calls for service, etc.). We also have several hundred corporate members, and we're reaching out to them as well—asking how we can help them in this changed world. We are not assuming that it's business as usual. We may have to significantly recraft some of our supplier-based revenue assumptions, and step up with new ways to serve these partners, as well as our individual members. We also have some major initiatives to provide resources to our individual members to demonstrate our commitment to help them be successful.

Janet G. McCallen, *CAE, Executive Director and Chief Executive Officer, Financial Planning Association, Atlanta*

We're not taking steps to retain members. In fact, we are setting and sticking to deadlines harder than ever before for dues payments and receivables. We look at it from a business standpoint and feel that in these challenging times, credit risk management is as important to us as it is to our member companies. We can't get caught out on a limb with uncollected receivables, nor can we afford to provide publications and services to companies that may not make it. When a member doesn't make a deadline, we resign them in a nicely worded note that explains that we're sorry to do it and we look forward to serving them again. It's worked well, in that it motivates many companies to pay and has weeded out the weaker ones.

Sid Smith, *President and Chief Executive Officer, The Hosiery Association, Charlotte, North Carolina*

We decided earlier this year to increase the emphasis on membership retention in 2002. At the end of 2000, we were at an all-time membership high and the retention dollars—and concurrent nondues income—were too big to continue to treat as a seasonal issue or part-time responsibility. On our small staff of 10, I had one person dedicated to membership recruitment and retention. Retention has hovered between 85 and 87 percent during the past 10 years, but now, increasing that percentage just one point is worth significant dollars.

In attempting to fill the membership position, I ended up with two excellent candidates. After apprising my executive committee about the opportunity to positively impact recruitment and retention by hiring both of them, I got the green light. My membership development director is now tasked with increasing the per capita participation in two key trade shows and our prepaid sponsorship program, and personally orienting every new member. She also makes personal visits and phone calls to improve retention. However the September 11, 2001, terrorist attacks affect the economy, our staff is more focused than ever on becoming a major business resource for our membership.

Mark P. Wylie, President and Chief Executive Officer, Associated Builders and Contractors, Inc. Central Florida Chapter, Winter Park

Recruitment: Know Your Budget, Resources, and Target Audience

The lifeblood of any association or non-profit organization is the members, donors, sponsors, and customers who pay dues, donate money, and buy products and services. More and more, nonprofit organizations are challenged to bring in revenue from an ever-increasing number of individuals, often with reduced budget or staff.

Before you begin your recruitment efforts, ask yourself three questions:

- What are my goals and objectives?
- Are the goals realistic?
- Do I have enough staff and time to achieve the goals?

Whether your association's budget is made up of dues or nondues revenue, your biggest obstacles to success are almost always limited time, staff, and money.

How much can you afford to spend on recruitment? Some associations are prepared to spend up to the first year's dues on acquiring a new member. Some allocate a fixed annual amount and no more. Both methods are widely used and work.

If your budget is tight, be creative in your approach to cut costs.

- What parts of the program can you scale down or do later?
- Are there other low-cost, free, or trade-out ways to reach your target audience?
- Do you work with vendor partners that, in return for mail house, production, or telemarketing services, could receive sponsorship at your next annual conference, free advertising in your newsletter or magazine, or some other benefit?

If you are in the middle of the budget cycle, and you are more than halfway below your target goals for recruitment, what can you do to ensure greater success? Everything you do should be put on paper and shared with internal staff so that everyone is aware of your expectations and your annual marketing plan.

Ask your vendor or marketing department if there are other ways to customize or produce your piece to bring the cost down. Just because you had planned to conduct your campaign a certain way doesn't mean that you shouldn't be flexible.

Ask members for testimonials and endorsements and assess their current or potential level of involvement in the association. The more you can get members involved, the more they buy into being a member or customer and, consequently, the more likely they are to renew their membership, make purchases, make donations, or serve as sponsors.

Members are valuable resources that you can use to draw others into your organization. Once you determine which members will be effective and what level of access they have to nonmembers, you can better target your prospect audience.

Who are the prospects you want to reach? Not every potential prospect is the same. Some will be easier to approach and more willing to join or buy; some may be too expensive or may be too time-consuming to recruit. In *Strategic Marketing for Nonprofit Organizations* (1995, Prentice Hall), Philip Kotler discusses three types of prospects: *resisters, indifferents,* and *uninforms.* Being able to recognize the attributes of these different types can help you better segment and target your prospect audiences.

- **Resisters dislike the organization.** They may disagree with the organization's principles or feel that the organization doesn't do any good. If these views are unfounded and the association can refute the negative impressions through well-founded evidence, you may be able to recruit some of these

Reprinted from *Membership Developments* ASAE newsletter, December 2000

Adapted from "Recruitment Techniques" by Lauren L. Corbin and Richard P. Whelan, from *Membership Marketing,* edited by Susan Nicolais, CAE, (ASAE, 2000).

individuals. But if these views are well-founded, then the organization will gain little by pursuing this group.

- **Indifferents are prospects who don't see much benefit to joining the organization.** The typical response you hear from this group is: "The dues are too high relative to the benefits that I would receive," or "I can get that benefit from other associations or organizations." This group includes *free riders*—people who feel that they can get the benefits of membership without joining. The best approach to indifference is to demonstrate that the organization's value is high in relation to the dues.

- **Uninforms are prospects who have little information on which to base a judgment.** They are the ones who say: "I really don't know what you do," or "I have no idea of the dues, but I think they are high." The best way to approach these individuals is to send them information to increase their knowledge of your association.

Just as your current members and customers have unique and specific wants and desires from your organization, new prospects and customers will have a variety of views and wants. You need to know who's who in your target audience and approach each group somewhat differently to better ensure success.

Dues Restructuring: Developing a New Model Reflective of Industry Change

By Marsha L. Turner, CAE

Reprinted from

Membership

Developments,

ASAE newsletter,

June 2001

Astate trade association for home care agencies, the Illinois Home Care Council (IHCC), Chicago, receives the majority of its funds (67 percent) from membership dues. In the years following the passage of the 1997 Balanced Budget Act, IHCC's dues revenues decreased sharply as many agencies were forced to consolidate or close.

Because IHCC uses a revenue-based dues structure and a sliding scale that invites members to pay less, it was no surprise that as members' revenues decreased, so, too, did the council's.

The sliding scale structure—based on a quantifiable measure such as revenue, number of employees, or units sold—is not uncommon to trade associations.

When an industry is healthy, a sliding scale benefits an association, allowing it to capitalize on members' good fortunes; member growth leads to the association's growth.

Conversely, it has a negative impact in a period of industry turmoil or downsizing, as members slide down the dues scale. Even with less money coming in, associations are expected to maintain the same level of service for the same number of members. This was the situation facing IHCC.

What to do?

Having made considerable cuts in staff, expenses, and operations and looking ahead to yet more industry upheaval, IHCC's board realized that drastic measures were required to keep the organization viable.

Any solution, however, could not place additional financial burden upon already-strapped members. Indeed, IHCC needed to offer some ease for members, particularly those challenged with immediate solvency concerns. Accordingly, the board appointed a representative task force to study the sliding scale structure and seek other alternatives for assessing member dues.

Developing the new model

IHCC wanted a dues model that would allow for new membership categories consistent with the board's long-term objective of expanding the membership base beyond Medicare-certified home care agencies. Important that it strike the appropriate balance between dues and members, the model needed to be:

- responsive to provider needs,
- flexible enough to allow expansion and growth, and
- fiscally responsible to ensure the financial solvency of IHCC.

The task force was given two guidelines:

1. Look outside of the long-accepted norm of the sliding scale.

2. Consider an assessment mechanism with greater stability than revenue.

After extensive research, the task force developed two new dues models. Based on IHCC demographics, and to ensure minimum revenue, both models were designed to assess the FY2001 base dues amount.

Model 1

Model 1 is component-based. To determine appropriate assessments for each component, the task force looked at current member product line demographics and calculated how many members claimed business in each component area. Then it determined base dues amounts for different types of providers, and component add-on amounts.

Under this model, for instance,

- a provider pays the appropriate base amount, regardless of revenue, and
- a provider with an add-on component pays the base amount plus the component cost.

Strengths. Fair and flexible, this model addresses the argument that the larger agencies subsidize the smaller ones, and it allows for growth in other untapped markets. Revenue verification is no longer a material concern.

Weaknesses. The smallest providers would see their base dues increase. While not a large dollar amount, member feedback told IHCC that this could be a problem for many smaller providers and could well become unaffordable should that provider have other components.

At the same time, there would be a decrease in what larger agencies currently pay. Many larger agencies have multiple components, but large providers could choose to register a single component that would yield the lowest membership assessment. This would have an obvious unfavorable impact on association revenue.

To address these concerns, the task force refined the model so that home care providers with annual revenue less than a designated amount (with no add-on components) would pay the appropriate base amount only. In addition, for purposes of dues assessment, a member would be required to include all product lines in which they have an ownership interest.

For example, a health care system would be required to consider all subsidiary corporations in which they have an interest. A system with home health, durable medical equipment, hospice, private-duty nursing, and pharmacy all under separate corporations would be considered a single provider with five assessable components.

Model 2

The task force also considered a member-revenue-based model with fewer provider categories in the event that the board decided it was not yet comfortable with a non-revenue-based assessment. By reducing the number of categories, IHCC becomes less vulnerable to the revenue reductions of its members.

Choosing a model

The board is considering Model 1 as the best long-term solution for the organization. A momentous decision, the pros and cons are still under debate. On the pro side:

- IHCC becomes less vulnerable to the revenue shifts of members,
- here is the possibility of increased membership by providers who cannot afford our revenue-based system,
- it is easier to determine agencies and their related components as opposed to verifying revenue levels, and
- IHCC no longer will be handicapped by a dues structure that guarantees trouble in a period of upheaval and strife.

As long as care is taken to ensure a base dues-revenue level from the new model, the primary disadvantage appears to be the risk of changing.

Making radical change is a risk from several perspectives. It will need to be carefully sold to members. For some, dues will increase, which could be a problem for the affected providers. For others, dues will decrease, which could result in decreased revenues for IHCC.

However risky change may be, the current system obviously doesn't work. Although a new system might not work either, to continue along the same path invites certain disaster. Given the current industry environment, the IHCC board believes that not embracing change is the greater risk.

A Lifelong Commitment

Looking for a better way to retain members? Consider the lifetime membership option.

By Barry S. Eisenberg, CAE

Reprinted from
Association
Management,
March 2001

For most organizations, retention is the biggest membership challenge. Much of the literature about how to improve member retention focuses on the importance of establishing a meaningful relationship between the member and the organization; paying strict attention to the delivery of products that represent value for the dues dollar to the member; and providing world-class customer service.

Yet, even organizations that are able to emphasize these elements still face at least one formidable obstacle: asking members to renew membership.

If the organization's products and services satisfy members, they will renew a high percentage of the time—85 percent or more. But the falloff across time can be significant and the relative costs of acquiring a new member versus retaining an existing one are well known. Wouldn't it be better to ask that member only once, and then have a dues-generating member for life? The lifetime membership option (LMO) is one way to accomplish that.

What is a lifetime membership?

Many organizations offer selected members the opportunity to have their memberships extended for life. This typically applies to members who have reached a certain age (generally 65); been a member for a specified number of years (e.g., 20 or more); or served in a particular capacity such as president or board chair. Organizations refer to these classes of membership in different ways—lifetime, emeritus, or dues-exempt. These membership categories can be useful, but have limited ability to boost membership ranks or dues revenues because

- there is no special status associated with them;
- they are often equated with no payment of dues; and
- they are not made available to the entire membership, except at times designated by the leadership.

The LMO addresses these issues by outlining an approach that associations can use to create a new membership category available to all current members of the association as well as nonmembers who wish to join. If properly constructed, a LMO can provide a stream of dues revenue during a member's lifetime, and also allow associations to offer special status to members who wish to demonstrate long-term loyalty.

How does it work?

The LMO concept is straightforward: The member makes a one-time, lump-sum payment to the association and becomes a member for life. The amount of the payment depends on the member's age. Younger members pay relatively more, older members pay relatively less. There are no more renewal and reminder notices to send out, no more bills for the members to pay, and no more checks or credit card payments to process. The association takes that one-time payment, creates a type of accrual account, and uses the lifetime dues payments and generated investment returns to pay or credit that member's dues each year so that they are reflected in the association's yearly financial reporting as revenues from operations.

In generating lifetime payment amounts, the key variables that determine the lump-sum amounts, other than age, are the base-level dues amount, off of which the lifetime rates will be calculated, and the implied discount rate.

To determine base-level dues amounts, associations can simply refer to their current dues level for full dues-paying members, the average dues level paid by all members, or a somewhat lower rate that reflects expected savings from the reduced administrative and processing costs. One logical approach would be to use the current dues level, but to reduce that by the anticipated administrative savings of the program. An association may find that when it adds up the costs of renewal mailings, processing, commissions, and so forth, this approximates 10 percent of the basic dues level.

Associations might also want to increase the base dues level to cover the additional costs of serving members in their later years. The higher the base dues level, the greater the lifetime payment amount. This base dues level amount represents the dues amount per member that will be realized in the association's operating budget on an annual basis.

Associations also need to select a discount rate. The discount rate, in this context, is an estimate of net investment returns that the association expects to receive from the lump-sum payments set aside in the accrual account. A conservative rule-of-thumb is that the discount rate should approximate the yield on the 30-year United States Treasury bond. If the discount rate is set at this level and investment performance exceeds that of the 30-year bond across time, the accrual account will generate excess funds that can be used for other purposes. The higher the discount rate, the lower the schedule of payments will be for the potential lifetime member.

Once the base dues level and discount rate are selected, a discounted cash-flow calculation (available in most computer spreadsheet programs) will generate the lifetime dues payments. These payments need to be tested against what it is believed that members might reasonably afford, and adjustment to the base dues level or interest can be made accordingly.

Associations can organize these payments year by year, or group the payments into segments of 5 or 10 years based on the age span of the membership. There isn't a great necessity for detailed actuarial projections because most membership organizations have self-imposed dues-exempt age limits (e.g., 65 or 70). Actual projections become necessary when there is no set dues-exempt age, as the member's life expectancy becomes a significantly more important variable.

To calculate the lifetime dues payments, determine:

- at what age your members currently stop paying dues;
- your base-level dues amount; and
- your implied discount rate.

Any association can tailor this basic calculation protocol to its particular dues or benefits policies. Allowances can be made, for example, for special dues discount programs already in place, or in instances when benefits tend to be reduced after a certain age. Part of this program's attractiveness to members is its simplicity, so it is preferable to keep complicating factors (and the generation of multiple payment schedules) to a minimum. It's best if these programs are nontransferable with a no-refund policy.

One additional variable to consider is the threshold for the LMO. The threshold is the additional criteria for a lifetime membership, if any, beyond an association's usual criteria for membership. An association might have no threshold, and thus accept any qualified applicant as a lifetime member. However, longtime members, who are likely to be the early adopters of the LMO, might prefer that some level of membership history exist before a member can purchase a lifetime membership. Such a requirement (e.g., five continuous years of membership at any level) would further emphasize the elite nature of the LMO.

Participant perks...

Members can enjoy great benefits from the LMO. The first benefit is obviously dues savings. Depending on the base dues level and discount rate, members can experience significant savings during their lifetimes. A conservative set of assumptions might produce dues savings of 60–70 percent.

The second advantage is convenience. The member makes a single payment and never worries about dues solicitations, check writing, or record keeping again. A third benefit is status. Associations can link the lifetime member with special status within the organization. Associations might even create an additional level of benefits available only to lifetime members.

Finally, the member may receive a tax benefit, depending on the association's tax status and whether the dues are paid by the individual, a professional corporation, or a business as a benefit of employment. Members may want to solicit professional tax advice before making any decisions.

...association advantages

Associations may accrue significant benefits from this program as well. Without question, it will improve the membership retention rate—the degree depends on the percentage of your members who choose the lifetime option. Assume, for example, that after three years, 10 percent of your members opt for this program and that your total membership is 3,000. If you normally achieve an 80 percent retention rate (considered good by national standards), this program, other things being equal, will boost the retention rate by two full percentage points—a significant increase.

Along with this improved retention rate comes the benefit of dues revenue stability, as the accrual fund will generate a guaranteed revenue stream. The program also offers the potential for revenue growth, even without an increase in membership. This can happen because members previously considered dues-exempt might be generating a stream of dues revenue long after the contribution would have otherwise dropped to zero.

A lifetime membership program also helps align the association's benefits with the members' benefits. The association gains by providing this option to its most loyal members, rather than by incurring expensive and unnecessary marketing and dues-processing activities. At the same time, by publicly recognizing the lifetime members, the association is both projecting status on these loyalists and calling on lapsed members, potential members, and the public at large to see the association's value.

The LMO can also be a potent product and marketing tool that emerges directly from the association's own dues structure.

Marketing makes a difference

As with any membership program, marketing is a key to success. Good marketing is critical with the launch of a program like the LMO when members are being asked to make relatively large dues payments. Plan to devote considerable effort to communicating and explaining how the program works and to continue this promotional commitment for several years.

It's important to recognize at the outset that this program will not be equally attractive to everyone. Some members may simply not have the resources to commit to such a membership program and others may be hesitant to make a lifetime commitment to one organization. In fact, the way the lifetime dues generally work out, the program may at first seem most attractive to older members. This group has the most history with the association, the lump-sum payment will be the lowest, and they may be anxious to gain the stature that lifetime membership connotes.

The LMO presents a great opportunity for creative, out-of-the-box marketing approaches. Lifetime membership can make a wonderful gift for families or friends to bestow upon new entrants into a profession. Companies that hire professionals in a particular field can offer a lifetime membership in the individual's professional association as a recruiting tool in a tight labor market. Corporate sponsors or foundations may want to award lifetime membership to individuals who achieve certain stature or make recognized accomplishments in the field.

Risk factors

Introducing a LMO is not without risk to the association. As with the introduction of any significant dues program, the association must assess the risks carefully. One risk is that once an association sets the payment amount, members who join under that amount are locked into a base-level dues rate. This is a great advantage for the member because it effectively protects them from the advent of future dues increases.

However, from the association's perspective, overall dues increases may become more difficult in the future. If a certain segment of the membership is locked out of dues increases, the needed relative increase for the remainder of the membership might be higher than would be financially or politically acceptable.

Another risk is that an association may select the wrong discount rate. If a higher discount rate is selected initially, it is possible that the accrual fund will not generate sufficient returns to fund the yearly dues payments. A third risk is that the association may set up the accrual accounting mechanism improperly and end up spending too much of the lifetime membership payments. This would involve a possible liability for the association that may be difficult to remedy.

All of these risks can be minimized through careful planning and close monitoring of the program in the early years. And just like any dues policy, associations can always choose to alter the dues payments in later years for new lifetime members if the system is financially underperforming.

The LMO is an excellent option for individual membership associations seeking to improve their retention rate and looking to add long-term stability to their membership dues revenue stream. Associations can implement a lifetime program in conjunction with other membership programs and present it as an option to current and prospective members. With proper leadership and marketing support, the LMO can become an integral part of an association's membership benefits package.

Installment Dues: An Option Worth Exploring

By Nancy Perkin Beaumont, CAE, and Chuck Martin, CAE

Reprinted from
Dollars & Cents,
ASAE newsletter,
September 2001

If your professional association has members who regularly bemoan the cost of annual dues, you may want to consider offering them the option of paying across an extended period of time with a credit card. Before you discount this option, consider the American Physical Therapy Association's (APTA) ongoing installment dues program.

When Congress passed the Balanced Budget Act of 1997 and the Health Care Financing Administration implemented the Outpatient Prospective Payment System, many physical therapists and assistants experienced lower reimbursement rates and reduced patient visits. As a result, many of our members experienced lower income levels and fewer benefits.

Furthermore, they began complaining about having to pay national and state dues in one annual payment, even if they could use a credit card and take several months to pay off the balance. Their pleas were heard, and APTA's House of Delegates asked staff to look at options for providing an installment dues program that would permit payment across a period of time while remaining revenue neutral for the association.

After some initial protest, staff explored various options and initiated a pilot test in five chapters. The trial allowed members to pay their national, state, and section dues, as well as foundation and political action committee contributions, across six months, with automatic bimonthly deductions from their credit cards. A commercial software package was used to handle the deductions, thereby minimizing hands-on staff involvement. The test was successful, and APTA immediately launched the program associationwide.

After the initial 25 percent deduction at the time of processing, APTA collects annual chapter and section dues across the extended period but transfers the full amount of annual dues to chapters and sections on a monthly basis.

To guarantee the program is revenue-neutral, the association includes a $15 handling fee to cover the slower cash flow to itself and to chapters and sections for dues revenue. To arrive at this sum, we used an estimated 7 percent *cost-of-funds* calculation together with some assumptions about how many members from each chapter would participate in the program. Annual chapter dues range from $50 to $245, so implications vary depending on a member's state of residence. Although we expected to hear many complaints about the handling fee, we were pleasantly surprised.

Our financial management system requires us to process dues in full. However, our accounting software handles the unpaid portion as accounts receivable, and a financial institution software package uses the initial entry to automatically prompt the subsequent three charges to a member's credit card. An Excel spreadsheet is used to record the monthly and cumulative activity by state, which keeps current participation rates readily available. APTA's independent auditors have reviewed the process and found it to meet their internal control standards.

Since its inception in October 1998, some 6,000 APTA members have participated in the program.

Leaders at the national, chapter, and section levels believe the program has increased membership and enhanced the association's reputation for member service. Complaints have been practically nonexistent, and staff who administer the applications have not found the process burdensome. The handling fee appeals to those who truly require the additional time for payment and provides nondues revenue to offset the costs associated with a slower cash flow.

In addition to the goodwill that this program has generated for APTA, it has also gone a long way in retaining and recruiting members during an economic downturn.

Value for Dues

Can you customize member dues based on return on investment? Here's how one association is making a value-based dues structure work.

By W. Henson Moore

Reprinted from
ASSOCIATION
MANAGEMENT,
June 2001

In my experience managing a trade association with corporate members, one thing became clear: Value or return on investment for membership dues is the most important factor in joining or remaining a member. It may be the only thing companies care about. With increasing cost-cutting pressures exacerbated by mergers and acquisitions, corporations must fully assess what it costs to belong to anything and what they get in return. At each annual budget exercise, the corporate CFO suggests to the CEO that leaving the trade association is an easier choice than closing a facility or letting employees go. From interaction with peers, it is a phenomenon we will all soon face if we haven't already.

Many of us have gone through our own downsizing, as our members have done, to reduce costs while increasing value. In 1995, we at the American Forest & Paper Association (AF&PA), Washington, D.C., cut our budget 28 percent and our staff 20 percent. Since then, staff numbers have remained level, and at $31.9 million, our 2000 budget was only slightly smaller than after our initial reduction for 1995. Nearly every association has probably tried to work smarter and to prioritize better to improve value. Likewise, under strict new budget procedures, we fund the highest-priority issues or activities first and fully, and then go down the priority list until our board-approved funding level is exhausted. Remaining issues are not funded.

As with downsizing, most of us have tried to do a better job communicating to our members the value we have achieved for them. At AF&PA, we quantify the dollars we save our 132 member companies, including 57 paper companies, 48 wood products and forestry companies, and 27 that are

both, and report it prominently in our annual report and by personalized letter. Yet with all of this, our members were still restless. To me it was clear: If getting lean, prioritizing, and improving communication weren't the solutions, we were encountering a new problem. I believe that value received or return on investment—not for the overall industry but for each individual company—may be more important than all other membership benefits put together. If the value is a great deal more than their dues, members are satisfied. If they think it is too close to call or less, they want out. Corporate members are now approaching association expenses as they would approach any other company expense.

Creating the framework

I decided we had to devise a dues system that tackled this problem. We started with the concept that all members do not receive the same value. After thorough analysis, this theory proved to be correct. First, we set up a cross-organizational team from our membership and economics departments who worked extensively with staff in each of our other departments. We began by examining in detail each issue and program we worked on. Then we determined how they affected each of our product segments. If an issue or program was highly relevant to a particular product, we reasoned that the companies making that product should pay relatively more of that issue budget. Based upon this analysis we constructed a new value-based dues system, which charges members for the value received rather than charging all members the same fee.

This system was met with acclaim by our members and was responsible for retaining several key members. Although some of our members initially thought the system was too complex, once we demonstrated how it worked, we gained their support. All agree it is a fair system. It is a bit more involved than charging everyone the same on a dollar of sales basis as we had done before, but it is much more equitable. The system is revenue neutral—it does not increase or decrease the total dues coming in; it just redistributes it by who receives value.

Assessing value

The first step, which began in late 1999, was to list everything we do—every issue, every service, every activity. We identified almost 40 separate programs and major issue areas that we work on and allocated our budget accordingly. Some of these issues, such as water quality, were more general in nature. Others were more narrowly focused large programs, such as our award-winning Sustainable Forestry Initiative (SFI) program. The second step was to assess all costs associated with each issue, including direct expenses and staff time. AF&PA's budget is entirely issue based, allowing us to examine budgets and expenses by issue rather than by department. Our staff also tracks their time spent working on these issues on a daily basis. We separately account for overhead expenses such as rent and administrative functions. These first two steps were not difficult and were objective or factual in their determination.

The third and final step was to go company by company to ascertain whether they received value from each activity listed. We began by gathering input from staff with expertise in those issues. These people were asked to determine how their issues affected each product line AF&PA represents. Once we had compiled those responses, we asked our volunteer member committees to provide feedback. We chose to go through our standing committees so that we could quickly reach consensus. For the most part our members felt the information we had collected from our staff was correct.

Assigning cost

This last step was a bit more difficult and approached subjectivity. It became obvious that some activities benefited a member fully, and others not at all. Those were easiest to assess. If designated a full benefit, the member paid its full pro rata share (based on its proportion of the sales of the members who also got full value) of that activity's cost. If no benefit was received, the member paid nothing for that activity. For example, if a company doesn't make lumber, it shouldn't pay for an industry program that promotes the use of wood products. This is not a cafeteria plan. A member may not choose whether or not to pay for activities for which it receives value. It pays for all areas in which it receives value and nothing on those that do not offer a return on investment.

The difficulty came in those cases where the member got some benefit, but more than some and less than others did. For example, since all members use wood fiber in their products, all receive some value from our SFI program, which ensures that our forests are managed correctly, thereby securing our raw material supply. Companies owning forestland and making products from the trees get the most value. Those that don't own trees but make a product from them get less. Others that don't own trees but make products from recycled paper get less still. All get some value, but not to the same degree.

To deal with this, we devised *relevancy factors* to assess what dues level would be charged members on a particular activity where there was a spread of value received. These factors make logical sense, but can be subjective. It would probably be impossible to create an entirely objective measure. The factors primarily set value received at five levels—0 percent, 25 percent, 50 percent, 75 percent, and 100 percent—for each member for each activity. We chose these levels because they offered enough variation to differentiate value, but not so much that it would substantially increase the system's complexity. If a member got no value, the factor was 0 percent; if the member received full value, 100 percent. Then subjective judgments were made if value was at neither extreme as to whether it was at the minimal level of 25 percent, or half as much as full value (50 percent), or almost at full value (75 percent).

For example, this is how the system would affect two products, corrugated boxes and lumber, under an issue like reduction of tariff barriers. Corrugated boxes are widely traded internationally and face tariffs in many nations. As a result, success on this issue would benefit this product and we would assign that product a relevancy factor of 100 percent. On the other hand, lumber is widely traded but faces much lower tariffs. As a result, a member's benefit from this issue is lower than that for corrugated boxes and we would assign it a relevancy of 50 percent.

Once the relevancy factor was set at a percentage level, say 50 percent, then dues assessed that member on that activity would be 50 percent of the dues rate on member's sales, or half what the rate was for a member who got full value (100 percent). While this sounds complicated and appears subjective, our experience shows that agreement can be readily reached on what level of value a company receives for a particular service or activity. Each year we review the relevancy factors with our member committees to ensure that they match the work we are doing. All requested changes are reviewed by the CEO membership committee for recommendation to the board.

We did not forget overhead or the core costs of running an association, which include such things as rent, insurance, taxes, administrative staff, and other administrative costs. These costs could be apportioned to each activity, or kept as a separate category. We chose to place these costs in a separate category to represent the expense of keeping the doors open. After nondues revenues were factored in, these overhead costs represent a 14 percent surcharge on each company's dues bill.

To put all this together, staff designed a computer application to merge the cost of each activity with the relevancy factor for each member for each activity and to compute the resulting dues. A detailed one-page printout serves as an invoice, but also effectively reminds the member of what it is and is not paying for. This ties dues directly to the value received. It is now easy for a member to see exactly what it is getting for its money.

Testing the waters

Our pilot program, which we conducted in 2000, involved two of our product lines where we faced the greatest challenge. The pilot provided invaluable data that has helped staff to fine-tune the new dues system. Even though the pilot focused only on product sales without accounting for acreage, raw material consumption, or pulp production, we found that we needed to include those additional factors. Two companies might make the same product, but the value they receive from AF&PA varied greatly depending on whether they owned forestland.

Reassessing value

Obviously, this is a system that must be able to incorporate change at least on an annual basis. Some activities will be dropped and are replaced by new ones. Others are reduced or expanded in scope. Members may change through mergers, acquisitions, or by adjusting their products or production processes. The dues system must be able to account for these factors and adapt. Otherwise, the basic complaint of lack of value or return on investment may reappear. We have chosen to review these, as well as the relevancy factors, annually through our member committees as part of the budget process. Our members now play a more active role in that process as they simultaneously review the activities, their cost, and the relevancy factors for each issue.

Garnering support

At first glance, it may seem that convincing the board and membership of this system's logic and utility would be a difficult task. We first built support within a CEO membership committee. Once we had this group's blessing, we approached those companies that would see a significant increase under the new system to gauge their reaction. Once we fully explained the system, we encountered no major objection, which led us to seek board approval. In May 2000, the board approved the new dues structure and implementation began January 1, 2001.

Business is changing and most experts think that changes yet to come will be even more rapid and profound than we have ever experienced. We are also facing competition in the association business not only from other nonprofits, but Internet for-profits as well. The resulting pressure is recognized by all of us in the association profession who represent business. We certainly have to be leaner, more effective, and better communicators than ever before, but I think we also need a dues system that is based on what matters most to our members. I believe this is key to our future and in turn, to our members' futures.

When the Going Gets Tough, the Tough Go Online

Reprinted from
*Membership
Developments,*
ASAE newsletter,
February 2002

By Deb Tompkins

Membership directors and their marketing teams are experts at getting results on shoestring budgets. Still, they do most of their membership marketing through the mail or over the phone—the two costliest direct-marketing channels. With budgets strained and direct-mail response rates declining, there's never been a better time to try migrating membership marketing online. Here are five marketing strategies that take advantage of the Web.

1. **Ask your members to refer their colleagues online.** Traditional member-get-a-member campaigns are so labor-intensive that only a handful of members actually participate. Instead of asking your members to recruit their colleagues, ask for the names and e-mail addresses of potential candidates for membership. By making it easier for members to recommend your association to their friends, you'll increase participation and collect significantly more membership leads. Send a series of e-mails to these hot prospects, linked to your online membership application.

2. **Use e-mail *auto-responders* to turn Web buyers into members.** If your Web site sends automatic thank-you e-mails to confirm publication sales or conference registrations, rewrite the message to reinforce the value of membership. Remind members how much they saved, and invite nonmember buyers to join and lock in future savings. Or take it one step further, and offer to discount the recent purchase at the member rate if the prospect joins within a certain period of time.

3. **Add a membership offer to every online sale.** While we're on the subject, why not ask nonmembers to join *before* they purchase books or register for meetings? Adding a membership offer to Web forms costs practically nothing. Or create a pop-up window that opens only when the buyer selects the *nonmember* option on the form. The window highlights member discounts and tells the buyer how to join and lock in lower member rates on the current purchase.

4. **Try an early-renewal e-mail with a special offer**. Members who've renewed three or more years in a row will probably renew again this year. Why wait to collect their dues? Use e-mail to confirm their renewals early. Link to a special renewal page where the member can give you a credit card number or request an invoice. For a softer offer, delay charging the card until your regular renewal cycle—and still save the cost of sending multiple notices.

5. **Use banner ads to push membership and renewal.** Placing banner ads on your Web site is a great way to push visitors to your online membership application and renewal form. Examine your Web usage statistics to see which pages get the most traffic. Develop a banner ad (hint: text-only ads outperform flashing banners) inviting prospects to join and current members to renew.

Blend these five cost-effective, integrated marketing ideas into your traditional acquisition and retention mix—and save your shoestring budget for other expenses.

Copyright 2002, JAM Communications, Inc. Used with permission.

Marketing and Advertising

Letter From the Chair: Sweet Marketing Ideas for a Sour Economy

By Rick Whelan

Reprinted from
*Membership
Developments,*
ASAE newsletter,
March 2002

Perhaps we should reintroduce our membership and marketing professionals to the old adage about making lemonade when life hands you lemons. It seems now is an appropriate time to remind them that we are all counting on them to continue at perhaps a more serious pace than usual.

Every day brings a roller coaster of economic news. The stock market is up one day and down the next. Divergent views from just about every forecasting group out there will tell you whatever you want to hear about the economy, except one thing: when it will get better. And it *will* get better.

In early February, the *Washington Post* described our predicament in an article subtitled, "Nonprofits Face the Same Recession-Related Financial Problems as Their Members."

"The recession has hit Washington, D.C., nonprofit associations hard," writes Neil Irwin, who goes on to say that "the types of associations facing tough times reflect the economy as a whole."

That's true, and not just in Washington, D.C. Many associations, especially those representing businesses most affected by a recession—technology, travel, and manufacturing—are hurting, while some involved in security or human resources are having a great year.

In fact, for the Society for Human Resource Management, Alexandria, Virginia, fiscal year 2001 was one of the best membership recruitment years ever.

Plus, these smart folks haven't pulled back. Instead, they're looking for avenues of expansion in their marketplaces, such as businesses that may not employ a full-time human resources professional but still need help with HR-related questions. Likely candidates include small business owners and organizations with staffs under 50.

Membership professionals must find ways to work through the tough times. If your association is hurting, then you most likely want to stabilize both member counts and revenues in the short term.

For associations that represent those sectors of the economy that are down, now is probably not the time to plan big, expensive acquisition campaigns. Spend your resources on renewing or reinstating those members or customers you already have (or had) or on upgrading current members, if your dues structure allows it. Then try to get them to spend more money with your association, thereby increasing their lifetime value.

If you're in a sector that's doing OK, you most likely will want to increase market and customer share, perhaps even targeting the markets of some of your competitors who've pulled back their marketing efforts.

No matter what situation your association finds itself in, now isn't the time to go silent or necessarily do the same old thing. Take a look at what a few associations are doing.

• Those of you who know the nursing market know there are probably more nursing-related associations than there are nurses to join them. In response, the Association of Perioperative Registered Nurses, Denver, now offers the EZ Pay Dues Payment Plan, which allows new and renewing members to pay their dues in three installments with a credit card. This helps to make the decision to renew or join easier.

What's more, staff and volunteer leaders are rededicating themselves to actively stressing the benefits of membership, reminding members just what they get—both tangible and intangible—for their membership dues payment.

- The American Physical Therapy Association (APTA), Alexandria, Virginia, has seen a decline in membership, thanks in part to the tight economy. Instead of spending precious dollars on new recruitment, APTA has started trying to win back lapsed members who are familiar with the association but who, for some reason, have allowed their memberships to expire.

Results are just starting to come in, but the response rate is reportedly strong. Here again, an association returns to the basics of understanding the need to belong, especially in a time of heightened anxiety and economic strain. Associations offer tremendous *community* and access to job banks, networking opportunities, and continuing education.

Engaging Your Marketing Mind

By Michelle Poskaitis

Reprinted from
Marketing Fast Facts,
ASAE newsletter,
November 2001

*This article was
excerpted in part from
Smart Marketing for
Associations:
Marketing Plans That
Work, by Michelle
Poskaitis (ASAE, 2002).*

Strategic marketing is at once a business philosophy and a practical discipline of association management pervading every function of the organization with a focus on the customer and the world in which he lives. It requires clear understanding and articulation of the past and present as well as a forecast of what might happen in the future.

Strategic marketing is characteristically *outside-in,* meaning that your attention originates with the customer, not the association, ultimately helping you to create products, services, and experiences to ensure an ongoing, satisfying relationship between the two.

For decades, the four P's—product, price, place, and promotion—have served as the framework for effective marketing management. The blend of these four variables resulted in a marketing mix to form the basis of an organization's marketing initiatives. The four P's are

Product: products and services an organization produces and sells (because it can);

Price: the amount charged (to cover costs and make profit);

Place: where the organization distributes products or services (because they are the easiest and cheapest places to do so); and

Promotion: what the organization says about the product or service (to the masses whenever, wherever, and however they want).

This framework evolved some 40 years ago, in an age of consumerism characterized by *caveat emptor,* let the buyer beware.

Today, organizations need to adopt the four C's—customer, cost, convenience, and communication—in framing strategic marketing initiatives to achieve organizational objectives. Coined by Robert F. Lauterborn, co-author of *The New Marketing Paradigm: Integrated Marketing Communications* (NTC Business Books, 1997), the four C's encour-

age us to operate our organizations from the customer's perspective. Lauterborn advises the following:

"Forget product. Study consumer wants and needs. You can no longer sell whatever you can make. You can only sell what someone specifically wants to buy."

"Forget price. Understand consumers' costs to satisfy their wants or needs."

"Forget place. Think convenience to buy."

"Finally, forget promotion. The word is *communication."*

Lauterborn's approach isn't a marketing fad. It's a fundamental shift in management philosophy and practice, primarily in response to dramatic changes in how people decide to purchase. So, while the product or service is an essential ingredient, it's pointless without a customer. Pricing affects profits, but only to the extent that the customer will buy at your price points. Therefore, your pricing needs to consider cost recovery as well as the customer's intellectual, emotional, and sensate response to paying the sales price.

With the Internet and increased competition, availability of comparable products and services is infinite. How convenient do you make it for customers to acquire your products or services? Are your publications available on your Web site, at your annual meeting, and from other sources?

Fifty years ago, mass marketing worked. Promotion focused on mass distribution of the same message. Since then, consumers have grown up in a culture pervaded with media. Today, old and young alike are inundated with advertising messages. Like any long-term relationship, two-way communication is essential. In today's economy, it's too easy for customers to take their dollars elsewhere.

The marketing mindset

Successful marketing is not a random phenomenon. People who consistently win aren't lucky; they make it happen. In addition to being creative, strategic marketing requires you to be

Analytical. You must find, face, and act on the facts and logical assumptions of the market environment; target audience; available budget; and other opportunities, limitations, and resources that converge to form your association's present reality. You'll also need to experiment and embrace the lessons learned from each success and failure.

Collaborative. Marketing is an integrated business discipline that affects and requires input from every area of your association. You cannot do effective marketing alone. Whether your association operates a centralized or decentralized marketing department, those responsible for the marketing function need the wisdom, resources, and cooperation of all stakeholders—especially co-workers, service providers, strategic partners, and customers—to accomplish the association's goals. Collaboration and open communication ensure credibility and buy-in from your colleagues.

Curious. Effective marketing requires a wholesome, eager desire to learn and be informed by customers, competitors, market opportunities, new strategies, successes, and failures. It asks you to consistently strive for a 360-degree view of a moving target, to observe as an enthusiast in the bleachers, a coach along the sidelines, a player on the bench, a reporter in the media box, a fan tuning in for the play-by-play, and a team player who scores the winning goal.

Flexible. As markets evolve, you need to meet your customers where they live, work, and play. As products and services age, you need to redesign, repackage, or retire. When operations break down, you need to adjust people and priorities. You need to bend—and even contort—without breaking. Sometimes that means going with the flow. Sometimes that means interrupting and redirecting the flow. Other times that means turning a program upside down for a new perspective. However you and your organization choose to achieve it, flexibility is essential.

Committed. It takes time and constancy to nurture and sustain profitable relationships with prospects and customers. Big goals require sustained, collaborative action, and most strategic marketing initiatives demand more than 12 months to mature and become fully productive. You must think and act in the long term while reaching short-term milestones that consistently move the organization toward a desired future.

Pick Your Niche

By Peter Wacht

Reprinted from
Communication News,
ASAE newsletter,
March 2001

Associations rarely have the resources that they need—money, personnel, or time—to put as much into a public relations campaign as they'd like. Despite competing priorities and deadlines, you need to develop a program that meets the needs of your association, whether it involves introducing a membership recruitment effort, a new book for sale, or a government relations initiative.

How can you succeed? Pick your niche. For the past two years, the National Court Reporters Association, Vienna, Virginia, has attempted to recruit more students into the profession. With a limited budget, we have focused on several key niches to get the word out.

One of our most effective strategies was targeting career columnists across the country. Working with our public relations counsel, we submitted press releases consistently to our mailing list of 400 career editors, columnists, and Web site editors. Our efforts led to more than 200 clippings in the past two years in publications such as *The Washington Post, The Los Angeles Times, The Denver Post,* and *The Atlanta Journal-Constitution.* We also included our information packet in the material sent out by the Associated Press's career editor to its 1,550 member daily newspapers across the United States. The cost was low; the resulting exposure was great.

Niche isn't about size, it's about focus. Here are a few tips for running a niche-oriented campaign.

1. **Select only those niches that relate directly to your public relations effort.** If you're introducing a new program that benefits a specific subset of your membership, target those members. Don't waste your time or money marketing to the entire membership.

2. **Determine what works best for the niche.** Does your audience prefer press releases, e-mail, or personal contact? Career editors prefer information that can be easily reworked into their columns or publications. If you're promoting a book to an outside audience, keep in mind that many reviewers prefer a basic information sheet and a review copy of the book. Give them what they want.

3. **Keep your message simple.** Our message was clear: Court reporting and captioning are high-tech professions that offer challenging, exciting, and high-paying careers to the right people. In every contact, we mentioned that more information was available on a Web site (created specifically for this purpose). Since the start of the campaign two years ago, we've averaged more than 4,200 visitors per month.

4. **Be consistent with your efforts.** Marketing to a niche is similar to advertising—the more a consumer sees an ad, the more likely he or she will recognize it. The same applies to public relations.

5. **Stay focused.** Once you've developed your public relations campaign and selected the appropriate niche, stick with it. If an opportunity arises to obtain additional exposure in another area or niche, don't jump at it unless you're certain that the possible results will be worth the time and effort.

Getting the Budget You Want

Reprinted from

Marketing Fast Facts,

ASAE newsletter,

April 2002

By Karen G. DeLong, CAE

Frustrated by small expense budgets and big income goals? You're not alone. In many associations, the marketing budget is the first to get hit with cuts. So what's a marketing professional to do?

If your association operates on a calendar year, you may think there is plenty of time to prepare for the next round of budgeting. However, taking care of some important homework now can make your job easier when it's time to start crunching the numbers. You can get the information you need to build a strong budget with justifiable numbers. Here are some guidelines to help you get what you want.

1. **Study your association's marketing budget history.** Start on a macro level: What has your association spent on marketing in the past, and what was the association's income for those years? Look at individual program areas next: Can you find a correlation between dollars spent and income generated? For example, was membership income higher if more marketing budget was spent? If not, can you find out why?

2. **Spend time now developing systems to evaluate your marketing efforts.** To make a compelling argument about the money necessary to generate desired results, you must have airtight evidence of dollars spent versus dollars gained. Now is the time to work with your database and information technology colleagues to implement solid tracking mechanisms and reporting systems so marketing efforts can be fairly evaluated.

3. **Make big *wins* early in the year.** If the numbers don't look good early on, you may be subject to mid-year budget cuts. Look at what worked best in the past and front-load your marketing plan for success. Leave the experimental, out-there efforts for later in the year; now is the time to market your best products to your best customers.

   For membership marketing, that would involve going to your top 20 percent to 40 percent of prospect lists and former-member files. In publications, push the biggest sellers, and introduce your catalog to former buyers. If you have board- or senior-management-directed initiatives that are meant to fulfill certain altruistic goals (but are likely to be budgetary disasters), keep these figures separate from your other marketing efforts on any reports you present. For example, if your board wants you to save a seriously declining segment of members, report this income and expense as a special initiative.

4. **Develop a zero-based budget.** Don't just look at what you spent last year. Decide what projects will meet your objectives and get actual cost estimates from printers, mail houses, telemarketing firms, and other service providers. Keep these written quotes as proof that you're not just sandbagging the numbers.

5. **Attach your budget to the association's strategic plan.** If you don't have a strategic plan, go to your chief staff officer (or whoever will review this budget) and get a feel for his goals. For example, is it important to grow membership numbers or increase net revenue? Often, there is a big difference in marketing strategy depending upon the answer to that question.

6. **Illustrate the correlation between income and expense.** If you've done

your homework, history should tell you what percentage response rate to expect on various marketing campaigns.

For example, let's say you have 20,000 members and a goal of 10 percent membership growth. You will need 22,000 members at the end of the budget year to meet this goal. At an 80 percent retention rate, you will lose 4,000 members. Therefore, your true new-member acquisition goal is 6,000 members.

If previous membership campaigns average a 0.70 percent response rate, you'll need to reach 857,143 prospects to achieve 6,000 new members. Therefore, you would plan for that level of outreach when securing bids to develop your budget.

If your budget is cut, remind management of the consequences. Using the above example, cutting your acquisition initiative by 10 percent means outreach to 771,429 prospects, and only an estimated 5,400 members gained. At a dues rate of $100, that's $60,000 you'll have to cut from the income side of the budget projections.

7. **Cultivate marketing champions across the organization.** Often the marketing budget is cut because of a lack of appreciation or understanding. Offer to do a brown-bag informational seminar for the staff, or arrange special review meetings of marketing initiatives with key colleagues and other stakeholders.

Budget development is integral to creating the marketing plan. Start with a great plan and the steps outlined above, and you will have a road map for success across the year.

Advertising Sales in a Tight Economy

Reprinted from
Communication News,
ASAE newsletter,
March 2002

By Nancy Frede

Every salesperson knows how challenging it can be to sell advertising—even in a thriving economy. To succeed in these sluggish times, associations must concentrate less on their needs and more on what advertising and marketing represents to their prospects: a targeted marketing opportunity for suppliers that want a variety of ways to reach their members.

The following steps will help you think like your prospects, deliver marketing options to suit their budgets, and keep them coming back with frequency or for a combination of other opportunities, including your trade show, electronic newsletter, or magazine.

You are now entering the world of consultant selling. The more you understand your members and what they're seeking and buying, the more you can convey this as a positive to your advertising prospects.

A proper fit

Examine the demographics and buying patterns of your membership. If you don't have this information, consider conducting a survey or focus group to find out more about your members or readers. You'll need to know what specifically your members buy, whether they have purchasing or recommending authority, what their expense budgets are, and how they use their purchases. From this information you can understand your members' needs. You have now identified the most important element of why an advertiser wants to market to your members.

Before you call prospects, research where they market their products, their marketing messages, what audiences they target, who their decision makers are, and their expense budgets. Prospects' Web sites can answer lots of questions and clue you in on industry information and buzzwords.

When speaking with a prospect, ask questions and always listen to the answers. If your association offers the right fit, you can shape your marketing solution accordingly.

Otherwise, offer to refer the prospect to another resource. If the answers meet your demographics, you can offer niche-marketing opportunities. In a tight economy, this gives the prospect an opportunity to target market to your association members.

The next step

Now that you understand the prospect's goals, think about how your magazine, tradeshow, or other advertising opportunity can help her reach her goals. Create a plan that includes advertising in the appropriate publications, added visibility at the conference, representation in pre- and post-show magazines, membership list rentals, and broadcast fax and e-mail campaigns.

Remember, potential advertisers and sponsors want to:

- increase their visibility,
- generate greater share-of-mind for particular products,
- introduce new products with special images,
- showcase their specialties with invitations to product demonstrations,
- educate current and potential customers about products,
- enter new markets,
- generate sales leads,
- shorten their sales cycles by getting closer to potential customers,
- sell their products on site at exposition booths, and
- stay up with—or get ahead of—competitors.

Where do you find qualified leads for advertising? Consider supplier-members, past advertisers, list renters, and competitors' exhibitors and advertisers. Look to regional and national trade shows for exhibitors, advertisers, and sponsors.

To combat pricing obstacles, consider bundling an ad with another marketing opportunity to create a two-for-one that's cheaper than purchasing both items individually. Or, as a value-added benefit, offer reprints of an article within which a customer's ad is placed.

Always remember to thank advertisers. Do it when you receive advertising contracts and again at conferences, perhaps by offering framed copies of their ads to display in their booths.

The specific object isn't as important as the fact that you give your advertisers something in return for their support, which, with any luck, will blossom into a mutually advantageous partnership.

Reprinted from
Communication News,
ASAE newsletter,
February 2001

Creating a Video on a Shoestring Budget

By Leona P. Dalavai

If you're trying to jazz up a convention, an awards program, or a general presentation for your association, consider making a videotape. With careful research and planning and a qualified video professional, you can create an impressive video on a budget of about $500.

Our budget included production and editing, narration, and copies of the final video. Producing a video on a small budget requires more work, but the experience is educational, not to mention fun and challenging.

The main rule to remember in video production is that time is money. Keep it simple and you have a better chance of staying within your budget. Here are some general guidelines to get you started.

- **Select your video professional carefully.** Ask around for recommendations and check references. Don't be shy about asking for work samples. After you've made a selection, meet with that person and note your small budget up front.

- **Decide whether you are going to use video footage, photographs, or both.** If you use video footage, make sure that it's professionally produced. Amateur work requires more editing. If you use photographs, make sure that they are of the highest quality so they won't need to be reproduced, rescanned, or retouched.

- **Allow plenty of time.** From start to finish, it took us about three months to produce our video. If this is a first-time endeavor, be liberal with how much time you give yourself to gather photos or footage, write your narration, and produce the video.

- **Provide logos or other artwork to the video professional on a disk.** It's portable and easier to access.

- **Avoid using custom-written songs** because they are time and money guzzlers. Video pros have a library of music that they can use for the project. If you use licensed music, make sure that you pay the necessary fee to the American Society of Composers, Authors and Publishers, New York City. If the license is already paid for by the video professional, then you may not have to pay the ASCAP fee. But it's always best to check.

- **Keep your video short**—no more than 10 or 15 minutes. Obviously, the longer your video, the more time and money it takes to produce. Generally it's hard to keep a viewer's attention for longer than that time period, anyway.

- **Study other video scripts before writing yours.** Generally, each photo or video description should not exceed 10–12 seconds. The script must be tightly written but also entertaining. Through an ASAE e-mail list, I obtained some samples of video scripts and studied them carefully before getting my feet wet. Writing the script was the most time-consuming part of the video production because I made several drafts and revisions.

- **Ask a volunteer to narrate, practicing the script beforehand.** If you decide to use a professional, expect to pay about $150 per hour for narration fees.

Meetings

Defying The Meeting Gods

By Megan Dakake

Reprinted from

ASSOCIATION

MANAGEMENT,

June 2002

While associations have long depended on meetings for a sizeable chunk of their operating budgets, when a recession hits that conference revenue stream becomes more vital than ever—in spite of the fact that luring participants simultaneously becomes all the more challenging. *Convene* journal's 11th annual Meetings Market Survey (March 2002) showed that associations, on average, depend on conferences to provide 33.2 percent of their income. Moreover, this is nothing new: According to *Convene*, that figure has remained virtually unchanged since the publication began conducting the survey in 1992. ASAE's *Operating Ratio Report* shows similar results, based on data collected in 1999: 29.9 percent of associations' revenue came from meetings, according to the report. And while those figures have held steady over the years, the challenge of holding a successful meeting has only increased, even more so these past few months than in other recessions: September 11 stifled potential attendees' willingness to travel. And yet during a recession, when declining dues revenues often are the norm, most associations can't afford not to have successful, well-attended meetings.

Enter associations who have beaten the economic odds; that is, those who have managed to stage events that were not only judged successful by past benchmarks, but broke previous attendance records—some by going back to the basics, others by aggressively pursuing new opportunities. As these associations have shown, there's nothing like a little creative thinking to defy the odds.

A consistent location

Bigger and better than the last meeting does not always necessitate jumping around the country, according to Bill Stagg, director of communications, National FFA Organization, Indianapolis. FFA's conference, held October 2001 in Louisville, Kentucky, drew 46,557 attendees from around the world—100 more than last year. One thing that works in FFA's favor, says Stagg, is that it keeps its convention in the same city for at least a few years running. "So there is not a learning curve each year," he says.

With a staff of 99 and an operating budget of $21 million, FFA had held its annual meeting in Kansas City for 71 years, until it outgrew the available facilities. The association launched a nationwide search that resulted in a seven-year meeting contract. Stagg says that staying in one location for several consecutive years allows FFA to "profit from the experience base. This meeting needs a lot of space, and by the time you factor in the volunteers and the logistics, we don't want to reinvent the wheel each year," he says. Another advantage to staying in one city, says Stagg, is that it allows the association to sign multiyear contracts, giving it bigger bang for its buck. "We're able to negotiate rates for the facilities and the hotels and transportation support that we can only do if you're bringing that kind of business to a location for a period of time," he says. "You get a better buy, I think, when you have more years involved."

Similarly, the Chicago Dental Society (CDS), which has an operating budget of $6.7 million, has no doubt that it has remained successful across its 137-year meeting history by putting down roots in one city and staying. "There's no question whatsoever," says CDS Executive Director Randall B. Grove. "We have a tradition. If [the meeting] were to go to another city or state, I think it would be a very significant learning curve for us to handle the on-site requirements, as well as gaining attendees' reception that they need to come with us."

It should be noted that although CDS, with a membership of 4,000, is a chapter of the American Dental Society, its midwinter meeting is open to dentists around the world, bringing in a record 30,666 attendees at its most recent meeting. Keeping a fixed location encourages large drive-in attendance numbers from the Midwest states, but more importantly allows CDS's small, 15-person staff to handle "literally everything" as it comes up, says Grove. "The details are static, but we always try to tweak the meeting to work out any little kinks and give some innovation to keep it fresh for the attendees," he says. "Our attendance is based on reputation, tradition, the finest scientific programming, and the best exhibition—and providing the attendee with those features year after year. That's what sets us up for success."

Of course, many associations still find it lucrative to move meetings around to tourist hot spots, hoping to lure additional attendees based on the attractiveness of the venue. Case in point: the annual meeting of the National Osteoporosis Foundation (NOF), Washington, D.C., held in early March 2002 in Honolulu. "We were stuck at 600 for the longest time, even three weeks before the conference," says Michelle Horton, meetings manager of NOF, which has a staff of 32 and an operating budget of $9 million. But the numbers took a last-minute upward swing, even surging past the original projection of 1,200 to a final count of 1,567. Horton chalks the final tally up to the exotic locale of Honolulu.

"We found a lot of people came with their families," she says. "And we did have a lot of spouses who called and said, 'I saw this brochure in the mail; I want my husband to go.' So any angle is great. It was a great vacation site and I think a lot of people took advantage and made the best of it."

Sweat the details

"It's really about the product. [Attendees] have got to want to be there, and the product has got to be relevant for them—the meeting has to relate directly to their professional development needs," says Kevin Kruger, associate executive director, National Association of Student Personnel

Administrators (NASPA), Washington, D.C. That programming philosophy might not sound novel, but it helped bring in record numbers at NASPA's annual conference held in Boston in March.

One slight tweak for this year's meeting: NASPA, which has a staff of 15 and an operating budget of $3 million, has always included a career services function at the conference where candidates come to be interviewed by potential employers, but this year gambled a bit and decided to nix its normal $40 candidate participation fee. The move paid off, with a record 1,200 candidates registering for that portion of the conference, boosting total attendance to 3,665. In all, nearly 4,500 interviews were conducted at the career portion of the meeting. "It definitely got more people to attend," says Kruger. "And we still charged the employers, but more employers came because more candidates were coming. So it was one of those cyclical things that kind of fed upon itself."

NASPA's move to drop the fee suggests that creative tweaks such as repackaging offerings might go a long way in selling a meeting. The American Society of Health-System Pharmacists (ASHP), Bethesda, Maryland, also has done some creative packaging of its own, and it apparently has paid dividends. Martha Davies, director of meetings administration at ASHP, touts a combination membership and meeting registration as its key to roping in attendees. In response to the demand for a guaranteed return on investment, ASHP, which has a staff size of around 200 and an operating budget of close to $34 million, developed a program where a nonmember can become a member for free by paying the full nonmember registration rate. "That has been very successful for us over the years," says Davies.

Also important to keep in mind is that it's not just participants who want to see a return. Naturally, those who foot the bill—the attendees' employers—have to be drawn in, too. "People are taking more seriously what they can get out of meetings and also have a desire to prove to their management that this is a viable, valuable thing to pay for," explains Patty Quinlan, director of meetings, Produce Marketing Association (PMA), Newark, Delaware. Also note that PMA took care in designing its meeting according to its members' wishes. "The feedback we get is that they want to have bigger-name speakers because they think it would enable them to sell it to their bosses," she says. In response to their members' requests, next year PMA, with its staff of 73 and operating budget of $12 million, is planning to break with their tradition of using lesser-known but strategic industry speakers by bringing in author and speaker Tom Peters as a keynote.

Getting the word out

Not surprisingly, marketers of meetings found themselves in a catch-22 earlier this year when association budgets were taking a beating along with the economy. That, of course, meant that meeting marketing budgets were being slashed as well—all at a time when meeting attendance was on the decline. "In 9 of 10 cases where attendance and exhibit sales were on the downhill slide, marketing expenditures followed," says Bob James, managing director of the Frost Miller Group and coauthor of *The Art of the Show,* which was to be published in April by the International Association for Exhibition Management. "But arguing with an organizer that marketing cutbacks are counterproductive in the face of decreased registrations and sales is hopeless. It's easier to squeeze water from a stone."

If your association has to make every dollar count, James recommends the following in order to avoid "silly, but all too common, marketing errors":

- **Schedule your event clear of competing ones.** Not doing so is courting disaster, says James. Why make attendees and exhibitors choose between events?
- **Promote to your attendees frequently.** Three direct mail hits should be your *minimum.* Time-starved attendees need reminders.

- **Put yourself in attendees' shoes.** You have to know what keeps your attendees up at night—and address those issues with your event.
- **Deliver quality—and deliver what you promise.** Underwhelmed by the content of meetings, attendees will disappear; unimpressed with attendance, the exhibitors will follow. Especially for the sake of next year's meeting, don't promise what you can't deliver.

Stingy marketing budgets

The dilemma of whether to either err on the side of fiscal caution by scaling back or to go forward with full-scale marketing campaigns has left many associations in a quandary. Nevertheless, some budget-conscious associations have thought creatively and ended up with win-win solutions. CDS secured the best of both worlds for its annual meeting in Chicago by producing a CD-ROM with the help of Proctor & Gamble and an underwriting grant. The CD, which included event information and a link to CDS's Web site with the ability to download the registration form, was sent not only to domestically based members who wanted it in that format, but to thousands of prospective attendees overseas, where shipping a paper publication would have been extremely costly. "We were able to put the program right in the hands of people throughout Europe and Asia at very little cost," says Grove. "It gave them everything they needed to know. The short-term benefit was certainly in cost savings because it could cost us anywhere from $15 per copy to get an almost one-pound publication across to Europe. And in the long term, I think we're building much more identity with many markets."

Scarce funds may have meant seeking out alternative communication vehicles for some, but for others it simply brought the pressure to make marketing messages resonate louder than ever with potential attendees in more traditional ways. NASPA's Kruger says that his association's message makeover entailed more explicit conference learning objectives. "We were clearer about how the content was going to be organized so that people were able to see their own special interests more clearly defined in the conference," he says.

NASPA took its clarity mantra a notch louder by posting the entire program online a whole four months prior to its conference, along with an itinerary builder. "We really expanded the kinds of information and ways in which our members can interact with the conference prior to the event—not just registering online, which is commonplace now, but having the entire conference program in a searchable database. This enabled people to make decisions about attending not just based on the theme, which is oftentimes all you get, but actually on the content of the programs," said Kruger.

After all is said and done, though, perhaps more important than the perks, the city, and the marketing is simply building a strong foundation of solid conferences across the years on which to stage a successful upcoming meeting. "If a name is synonymous with quality, they will come," says CDS's Grove. Kruger agrees, asserting that creating value for this year's meeting has everything to do with achieving a successful meeting next year. "You can have the fanciest marketing and all these great techniques to get them to come this year, but you've got to get them to come next year, too," he points out. You hope that you've got enough value in the marketplace that people won't opt out, but you never know. So you keep building that loyalty and that retention and willingness to come back every year. And you do all that by creating the best possible experience you can."

Tactics for Change and Reorganization

Anatomy of a Merger

By Bronislaw Prokuski

Reprinted from
ASSOCIATION
MANAGEMENT,
February 2002

As the familiar television ad goes: "Why don't we merge? I'm sure you'll love working for me." Despite this cautionary note, one need only peruse the daily financial pages to recognize that in the for-profit world mergers and acquisitions have been and continue to be a fact of life—directly or indirectly related to attempts to increase shareholder value. In 2000 alone, the Federal Trade Commission reported a record number of corporate mergers—more than 4,000 filings (required for each sizeable merger) were reported to federal antitrust agencies. While fewer statistics are available regarding association mergers, ASAE's 1996 *Policies and Procedures in Association Management* reported that 7 percent of the 1,572 association surveyed in 1995 indicated that they planned to merge with another association between 1996 and 1999.

There are good and bad experiences with mergers. As reported in the June 2001 issue of *CFO Magazine,* a study by KPMG, Inc., showed that of the 700 most expensive merger deals between 1996 and 1998, only 17 percent enhanced shareholder value—not a high rate for that measure of success.

While results of mergers vary, organizations continue to investigate their possibilities. So, it's not unlikely that the subject of mergers or affiliations may come up in your internal staff discussions or be prompted by your board. Alternative organizational structures—whether it be an integration, such as a full merger; an alliance or affiliation, where the branding rather than the legal corporate entity is retained; an administrative consolidation; or simply a collaboration—are being driven by technology, member expectations of greater value for less money, less seed money, industry niches no longer able to support multiple associations, decreasing financial health, or other reasons. These transitions to an alternative organizational structure can happen quickly or take

years, but in any case, they are not necessarily simple solutions or exercises. In fact, merging associations may be more difficult than combining companies, since associations have no equity ownership and are essentially bound to a network of volunteers.

The National Defense Industrial Association (NDIA), Arlington, Virginia, is a product of mergers and affiliations that have taken place since its founding in 1919 as the Army Ordnance Association. It became the American Ordnance Association in 1957 and then, primarily as a result of the number and breadth of its technical-oriented divisions, first merged with the Armed Forces Chemical Association in 1965 and then the Armed Forces Management Association in 1974. In 1973 it changed its name to the American Defense Preparedness Association (ADPA), again reflecting the broadened mission perspective. The '90s saw the affiliation of the National Training Systems Association with ADPA in 1992 and the merger with the National Security Industrial Association in 1997, the latter being the result of six attempts that took place between 1965 and 1996. Similar ventures continue and, as this article goes to press, we are close to announcing the affiliation of the Precision Strike Association with the National Defense Industrial Association, which became our organization's new name in September 1997.

Although a merger or affiliation can be driven as a consequence of the aforementioned considerations, the best opportunity for making such an event a success is to consider it as a sound business strategy before the need ever arises. Thus the exploration of opportunities where the strengths of two organizations can be built upon or complemented should be a part of every association's strategic plan. Some areas of consideration for identifying opportunities where combining organizations may be a good thing include:

- duplicate programs that can be consolidated;
- possibility for better value to be provided to members and customers through services, networking, and influence;
- business interests that complement activities, chapter initiatives, or other member service coverage;
- opportunity for market expansion with wider and more inclusive industry representation and strengthened advocacy position; and
- achievable cost savings through economies of scale, reduction of overhead, elimination of nonessential functions, or incorporation of new or improved business processes and procedures.

In testing your organization's compatibility with a possible merger candidate, consider other key questions.

1. Are your respective markets overlapping?
2. Is there geographic compatibility in terms of area of service?
3. Are the cultures of the organizations complementary—and do they provide growth opportunities or will they clash or be otherwise disruptive?
4. Are the respective assets of the organizations comparable?

With a long history of merger activity, the NDIA experience affords recommendations in the administrative and financial arenas that may be helpful for your organization if it chooses to pursue such opportunities.

Background basics

There are some overriding issues that drive the potential for overall success of merger activity, so a brief mention of them is in order.

First, a merger is like a marriage. On the surface, it may make sense to a lot of people, but one needs to question whether the underlying conditions are right. What is the culture and business philosophy? Looking at each of the parties in the potential merger, do the board management philosophy and level of involvement, the informal organization work ethic and attitudes, the attention to resource control, the commitment of management, and level of goodwill make for the right mix? Is there a powerful, sustaining impetus behind the venture that will help overcome the obstacles—real and imagined—that will undoubtedly arise? Be aware that no matter how hard you try, there will be victims of the merger.

Second, mergers are rarely a situation of equals coming together. Operating as such when it is in fact not a reality can delay decisions, hinder emphasis on important external issues, and contribute to the psychological costs of disruption, stress, and loss of productivity that accompany any merger. The question of "Who is in charge?"—that is, the selection of the new president or executive director for the merged organization—needs to be decided very early on, as situations involving co-leaders working together for any extended length of time tend to be fraught with disaster.

The role of association operations

Clearly, the administrative and financial areas are the hub or point of interaction for merger and transition activities and for the process actions—a point also where many of the stresses of the merger process first appear. The term that generally comes first to people's minds when considering a merger is that of *due diligence*—the care that the organization exercises to avoid harm to the organization or its resources and property. Careful due diligence is key in the decision to move to board approval of a merger. A simplistic view is that due diligence is a financial exercise, merely an examination of the books. In reality, it needs to be a thorough investigation of the overall business condition of the organization being considered, including the building of the business case for proceeding forward. Due diligence offers the opportunity to ensure that any cross-functional and transition activities are viewed by a joint-organization committee or process-action approach, and that all activities are thoroughly addressed. Everything from cancellation costs of duplicative commitments, insurance coverage, health and benefit programs, to results of membership surveys and actions of the board and executive committee needs to be reviewed. Due diligence needs to be a total exposé—because of the consequent legal and fiduciary ramifications and should be appropriately carried out by an independent, professional auditing or legal firm. The amount of time spent on due diligence relates to the thoroughness required by the staff and board in assuring the membership—and stakeholders—of the soundness and business efficacy of the proposed decision. That time can take a few days, a few weeks, or several months, depending on the type of association and the complexity of the organizations. Attention to a comprehensive due-diligence checklist (available from most audit firms) as part of the initial decision to even pursue a merger or affiliation will help all association functional areas and board standing committees, such as finance or executive committees, to familiarize themselves with and better address their responsibilities in the process.

Priority prep work

In the development of the business case supporting a merger, particular attention should be paid to nearly every aspect of your operation. Typically, NDIA conducts a thorough review of the following areas before getting serious about merger talks.

Financial operations. The merger of two organizations involves the merging of financial operations, budgets, and account structures. Hence, account definition, costing and allocation methodology, recurring and nonrecurring costs, and disparate revenue sources need to be considered. Forecasting the transition period and the future, or out-year, budgets for several years is critical to a sound business case. Key assumptions and their supporting rationale need to be developed relative to such items

as potential member attrition and disparate revenue sources. Rather than a discrete set of revenue and expense projections, a range for each year projected is more useful for presenting potential outcomes (in other words, base calculations on both optimistic and pessimistic scenarios). The assumptions should be documented with supporting rationale and presented in a consistent format such that variations can be easily effected and provided to the board in a timely manner for its decision making.

Human elements. The business plan needs to address not only the financial resources, but the human resources, as they are closely coupled. Staff reorganization, individual displacement, and loss of key staff can have a dramatic effect on the merged organization's capability to meet financial projections. Here are some actions that NDIA has taken to help with smoother transitions during mergers.

1. **Create a staff merger map.** A direct consequence of staffing concerns is the need for a staff merger plan that addresses the elements of structure, control, orientation, and training. These elements are a product of the organization mission, vision, and core competencies, all of which should drive the specific functional positions required. Typically a total combined staff reduction of 10–15 percent can be contemplated due to duplication, overlap, and relevance to new requirements. Therefore, your plan will need to address how you will effectively resize the new organization with appropriate attention to staff, member, and organization needs. Normal attrition may be a convenient solution, while deletion of unnecessary positions with an appropriate severance package another.

   If the merger proceeds, of course, the merged staff will need to know how the new organization will function. Essentially you need to provide them with the new rules of the road. All staff will have to have a knowledge and familiarity with what each heritage organization brings to the new mission capability, and all will need some element of training whether it be informal on-the-job coaching, or structured classwork on new systems.

2. **Pay attention to staff morale.** During merger planning and transition, special attention to staff sensitivities regarding the impending merger should be a daily activity. Acquainting everyone to the new mission and communicating up, down, and sideways to dispel fear, rumor, and doubt is key to each staff member's hierarchy of needs. At NDIA we've found a basic fact sheet, distributed by e-mail with a follow-up question-and-answer session with the entire staff, most helpful. The fact sheet covers the following issues:

- recognition of who made the decision to initiate the merger;
- explanation of why such a merger was conceived, evaluated, and approved;
- expected benefits of the merger to the organizations;
- articulation of the mission and vision of the new organization;
- date that the merger will take effect;
- name of the new organization;
- description and organization chart of the new organization;
- implications of the merger for the combined staff as well as individuals;
- revision or restatement of individual job assignments;
- distribution plan for organizational assets;
- composition of the new board of directors; and
- philosophy of the new entity.

The above list is not necessarily all-encompassing; tailor it to your specific needs, circulate the draft through your various departments to ensure its thoroughness, and pay attention to rumor control. Add items to the fact sheet as concerns or feedback develop. Be prepared for the sticky situations, as politics and culture will naturally interplay.

3. **Review revised benefits.** Employee benefits of the two entities need to be reviewed and estimates made for a new or harmonized program. Retirement plans should receive particular attention, given out-year liabilities and costs of termination, such as for a defined benefit plan if the choice is to move to a 401(k). You may also need to consider grandfathering in particular benefit coverage for certain staff. The overall task is feasible as long as your final program is equitable to all employees in its coverage—a set of options tables is generally sufficient for analysis and presentation.

Facilities considerations. As a part of your facilities review, you'll need to decide whether the current space and location(s) adequately provide for staff needs and member service requirements—the latter probably being the primary criteria. Selecting one location over another, incurring potential lease-termination costs, operating out of multiple locations, all moving to a new leased location, or building a new facility can all result in some significant transition costs. Ensure that they are appropriately reflected in the business plan for board approval and in your transition operating or capital budget. Consult early on with your property manager and agent—make them part of the decision team. You'll generally find their insight and market acumen invaluable.

During facilities review, you will need to give special attention to your communication, computer, and information management systems. Upgrading to a new baseline and standardization of operating systems, hardware, and software are priority decisions. Leasing or obtaining services from an association services provider should be in your decision tree. Get your information and communication services providers together as a group, make them part of the planning process, and get them to give you new insights on capabilities and options.

With all the advances in information technology currently available, the facilities plan for the new organization needs to consider the potential reduction in office space that can result from a well-conceived telework plan. A lot of your financial reports, meeting registration tasks, and other activities can be effectively and efficiently accomplished—with appropriate security safeguards—from a sufficiently equipped home office. Given that a large measure of association business is information related, with a great shift to the e-business side in the last few years, the positive aspects of teleworking for the employee can be effectively meshed with the organization's needs to better satisfy both. With e-business requiring both a 24/7 mind-set and operation compared to bygone days of 9 to 5, teleworking offers an attractive way to provide that needed operational capability. You may not achieve any major savings but you will probably do a lot for your participating employees' morale, particularly, for example, in large urban areas where commuting time and related expenses are substantial.

Supplier evaluation and other considerations. The merger period is an excellent time to build long-term support relationships with all your suppliers. And while we are mentioning suppliers, don't forget those that provide office supplies, printing services, and so on. The transition period can provide an excellent opportunity to renegotiate contracts or move to new suppliers with substantial savings given your new business volume.

A merger offers the opportunity to think out of the box on how to accomplish the association's mission, to provide new and improved service to members, and to do it with a reduction of costs—fundamental aims of any merger. All your overhead cost areas should get a thorough review, determining which activities continue to support your new requirements, can be made more

efficient, should be outsourced, or are no longer needed.

NDIA routinely reviews existing contracts with its own and the merger candidate's suppliers, allowing them to compete for the contract for the new organization. As a result of some of its merger and affiliation activity, NDIA has realized cost savings of 10–20 percent in telecommunication, printing, insurance, and other areas.

- **Legal and general counsel services.** Use a statement of work in your request-for-proposal solicitation and ask for information on knowledge and relevant experience, fee and retainer structure, work quality, withdrawal terms, and discharge provisions.
- **Audit services.** With the merger, you'll have exposure to at least three providers—those of both associations as well as the due diligence provider—so craft a statement of work they can respond to.
- **Payroll services.** If the merged organizations have been processing their own payroll, it's a good time to reevaluate to see if the new association's needs support the use of outsourcing as a more effective approach.
- **Banking and investment management services.** Chances are you'll have at least two suppliers to select from in each area. The time you need to spend on structuring a decision process for just those two can be easily expanded to include other sources. Use this as a ready-made opportunity to reduce fees and review your analysis reporting.

The list will go on depending on what other operations are in place—or need to be put in place. While the task may seem daunting, consider it an opportunity to take advantage of the intrinsic benefits of open competition.

Transition tenets

Well, you've done all your planning, the business plan objectives appear achievable, both boards have given approval, the certificate of merger has been issued, and now the actual transition-integration process is ready to begin. Now is not the time to relax, as the transition period is where all the good work beforehand can start to fall apart. The *diligence* part of your due-diligence review needs to be maintained. What was on paper now becomes reality and practice. Staff orientation and familiarization—preferably at a neutral, off-site location—should be the first priority. Senior-level commitment to making the merger work through retention of the best, coupled with a large measure of goodwill, must be readily apparent—with a consistent message maintained on a daily basis.

You will need to continually conduct process reviews by those directly involved in the specific functions and plan workarounds—remember you are now integrating a new range of cultures and implementation details may have been overlooked in some areas. Patience, persistence, and follow-up should be each day's game plan.

You might need to operate out of both heritage associations for a period while new facilities are made available, so communication and information systems connectivity

and associated costs should also be considered. Keep in mind that once the merger is announced and once you've started transition, member and customer communication and interaction with or *through one site* is a preferable solution even if only from a perception standpoint. Notwithstanding all the turmoil that may be going on in each of your functional activities, the merger transition needs to be seamless to your members and customers. Difficult, yes, but all aspects of your member and customer interface need to be actively thought out.

The specific time frame for the completion of an effective merger can vary widely—from three months to several years. Regardless of this time period, it is hoped, of course, that you and your members will eventually realize the expected outcomes that drove the merger in the first place. There is really no *cookbook* approach for success; much is dependent on the willingness of all parties to make it work. Having gone through several mergers now, we at NDIA have found the efforts both time well spent and a growth process that benefits all involved. We are now on to the next.

From the Listserver: Association Mergers

Reprinted from
Executive IdeaLink,
ASAE newsletter,
November 2001

Executive Management Section Council members monitor ASAE's section e-mail lists to respond to key management issues and to share responses or comments that section members may find of interest.

Question:

I'm looking at an opportunity (or maybe not an opportunity) to merge our automotive organization with another of like mission—somewhat different but not significantly.

What are some of the questions our board should be asking about this proposed merger? What are the pros and cons? It seems as though both organizations have been experiencing a decrease in membership and nondues revenue, which is why the conversation began. Also, how do the bank accounts merge?

Response:

The *Association Law Handbook* (ASAE, 1996), by Jerald Jacobs, has an entire section dedicated to this topic. It includes lists of questions to ask when either merging or consolidating associations.

Response:

Our association has successfully done what you are considering and continues to look for similar opportunities in the future. Among the categories of information, I'd suggest due diligence in the following:

- identity, membership value and benefit, and key membership programs and services;
- governance structure;
- audits and finance, dues rates (and any changes expected from the merger), outstanding debts or expenses, projected revenues and expenses, and taxes;
- legal—particularly articles of incorporation—bylaws, and existing, pending, or likely actions; and

- communication plan and schedule.

Don't overlook the importance of the last item. You can do all the due diligence necessary, and the merger can still crash and burn without a well-conceived and executed communication plan.

Response:

I have been involved with several mergers, and there are a couple of factors that kept jumping out as we worked through the process.

1. **Don't get lost in the minutiae.** Too often, boards or feasibility committees want to dive right in and compare one association to the other regarding issues such as dues levels, services, conference registration fees, and so forth. While the devil can most certainly be in the details, I have found that this means they are getting way ahead of themselves.

2. **Cultures.** To me, this is a critical aspect of merging. Can the cultures of the two organizations (and I don't mean just the staffs) really mesh? Are they sufficiently compatible now, and, if not, can the differences be worked out in the near future?

3. **Staffs.** This is a critical issue and is sometimes not accorded the respect it needs by the volunteer leaders of each association. In the majority of cases, people will lose jobs during a merger, and that is never a pleasant prospect. There is usually more attention paid to the ultimate roles of the two CEOs and less so to middle management and below. It can be traumatic for both staffs, lead to turnover during deliberations and before the actual merger is effected, and hurt morale. It is rare, though not impossible, for all staff to retain their jobs. Even if they don't lose their jobs, their roles may be altered—

and not necessarily for the better, according to those affected.

4. **Financials.** I have seen associations talk merger, and when it came to merging their finances, one or both parties balked. I have seen members walk away from the merger table because one party was kicking in only half the money that the other one was. Obviously, if associations are to merge, it is like a marriage. Both have to be willing to sacrifice to make the union work.

5. **Board makeup.** I've seen associations worry about who was going to serve as the merged association's first president, and ask questions about the remaining terms of board members in both associations. Are you going to double the size of your board to allow all existing

board members to finish out their terms? Will criteria be established to determine the composition of that first board? Or will a brand new board simply be elected at the outset?

Just try to cover all the bases, and handle the big-picture stuff first. Then, get into the details. If the major aspects can be agreed upon and the issues overcome, the details should follow.

Response:

There's a lot more to an association merger than merging the bank accounts. While there usually are a lot of complex technical issues to be addressed, mergers are always complex political processes. "The Road to Abilene," a recent article in *Executive Update,* the magazine of the Greater Washington Society of Association Executives, might help.

Office Space: Buying Versus Leasing

Reprinted from
Executive IdeaLink,
ASAE newsletter,
November 2000

Selecting office space is an arduous process for most associations, but deciding whether to buy or lease space does not need to be as difficult. Start by conducting a buy versus lease analysis to determine how best to proceed and consider the following questions:

- Where, geographically, can you best represent members?
- What tax savings will the organization qualify for?
- How much space do you need now and how will that change in the future?
- Does the association want to perform facilities management duties?

"Start with a team of staff and consultants to make important real estate decisions," advises Chris Murray, vice president of Gensler & Architecture, Design & Planning Worldwide, Washington, D.C. "This team should include legal, tax, and design representatives, as well as a real estate broker and association staff. The expertise each can bring to the table will speed up decision making."

Murray gives an example of an association that financed a new building with tax-exempt vehicles and chose to lease the extra space in the building. The attorney and tax consultants on that team advised that, in its case, the association needed to be quite selective with tenants in order to retain a tax-exempt status and benefit from significant tax savings.

The availability of funds is another important consideration. "Significant reserves or dues coming into an organization make it easier to prove to lenders that an organization can buy space. With less in reserves, leasing becomes a better option," says Robert Gottlieb, partner, Venable, Baetjer, and Howard, LLP, Washington, D.C.

Here are the pros and cons of buying and leasing for associations, according to these experts.

Buying

1. **Some association members prefer a headquarters building, and oftentimes, don't mind paying for it.** It's a tangible representation of the association and its mission. Gottlieb calls this "an association's trophy."

2. **Buying allows complete customization control.** If the association needs an auditorium or large meeting space, something not found in typical commercial space, or other uncommon amenities, it can be added. However, the ability to recycle this space, whether through sale or lease, can prove difficult with unusual amenities.

3. **In some parts of the United States, Washington, D.C., included, 501(c)(3) organizations can finance the purchase of a building with tax-exempt financing.** There are similar programs in Maryland and Virginia. Your bank can assist in putting these deals together. Murray adds, "Associations have the added responsibility of finding the best and most affordable funding methods when constructing a building. It's an obligation to its members to make the best use of funds."

4. **There is a definite economic benefit to owning an asset that will appreciate in value.** Depending on the economy, market, and geographic region, that appreciation could be significant, non-existent, or somewhere in between.

Leasing

1. **Buildings that can be retrofitted can be customized more easily and thus are more attractive for leasing.** Once you vacate, the burden of adapting the space rests with the landlord.

2. **Leasing allows for easier expansion or downsizing of space.** An organization can request expansion options and the ability to sublet while negotiating a lease.

3. **There are no facilities management duties to contend with when leasing.** If a property is owned, there is always some form of facilities management to consider, whether it's building maintenance or lease execution for unused space.

Having formerly owned its building, the Construction Specifications Institute, Alexandria, Virginia, decided to lease space last year. Tony Keane, deputy executive director, says, "We were tired of managing tenants in our building, so we opted to lease space in our new location. This gives us the flexibility to expand or downsize as needed. From an economic and strategic standpoint, owning does not make sense for us right now."

"There's a lot of movement in the market nationwide right now. So vacated space, which offers amenities and does not need a lot of customization, may be a good option. It's a good time to try to find some space that's easily adapted or fine as is," observes Gensler & Architecture, Design & Planning Worldwide's Murray.

Additional Cost-Saving Tips

The Top 10 Ways to Manage Yourself and Your Time

By W. Jan Austin

Reprinted from
AMC Connection,
ASAE newsletter,
September 2000

Feeling out of control and unable to manage one's time is a complaint of epidemic proportions. It's easy to see why when the pace of just about everything has increased, and unprecedented amounts of information bombard us.

Consider the following questions about you and your time:

- How do you wish to be in better control of your time?
- What benefits would there be for you in taking control?
- What is the feeling that results from not having enough time to manage your personal and work commitments?
- What's drives "busyness" for you?
- What happens when you attempt to complete a task while feeling pressed for time? Do any of the following sound familiar?
    - I exert a lot of effort but get minimal results.
    - I feel physical, mental, and emotional exhaustion.
    - I lack clarity and focus.
    - I feel unable to respond to other things in the environment.
    - I feel irritable and/or distracted.
    - I feel that the likelihood of my making mistakes increases.
    - I have minimal satisfaction with the task.
    - My time seems to fly.
- What are the consequences for you in your work and personal relationships if you are regularly caught up in a cycle of busyness? Many people report the following:
    - I appear frenzied, confused, not in control, and/or less trusting of others.
    - I may seem untrustworthy and/or unable to handle projects.
    - I may consistently fail to meet deadlines.
    - I appear to lack confidence and/or competence.
    - My relationships may suffer.
    - My performance may deteriorate.
    - My need to put out fires may obscure the bigger picture and/or priorities.

Manage busyness and the sense that time is out of control by following these 10 steps.

1. **Start with the recognition that you're not managing time.** You can only manage yourself (your attitudes, beliefs, and actions) within the flow of time. The experience of time has more to do with your thoughts than with clock time. The stress that you associate with time originates in your thinking.

2. **Prioritize your efforts.** Stephen Covey, author of *The Seven Habits of Highly Successful People,* makes the distinction between things that are important and things that are urgent. Most of the time, doing the things that are important, rather than the things that are urgent, results in greater effectiveness. Don't major in minor things.

3. **Do less to get more.** Economize your efforts. For example, when you're boiling a pot of water, you can fill the pot, cover it, turn on the heat, and let it come to a boil while you do something else—or you can stand there and watch the pot.

4. **Eliminate sources of adrenaline.** These are substances, activities, rela-

tionships, situations, or attitudes that result in your feeling charged up. Adrenaline can distract you from the focus needed to complete a project, increase feelings of anxiety, and intensify the feeling that time is flying.

5. **Eliminate things that are taxing your time and energy.** These are the situations, attitudes, or behaviors (in yourself or others) that you're putting up with that don't serve you or your larger purpose but consume physical, mental, and/or emotional energy. Eliminating them results in an increase in available energy for people and projects, an overall feeling of calmness, and more time.

6. **Simplify your environment.** Clutter in your office or home environment can create stress. It can feel like you have more work to do than you really have when you archive unnecessary things in your environment.

7. **Simplify your tasks.** This may involve over-responding and under-responding.

    - **Under-responding:** Example: a fax that needs only a quick response or a confirmation. You can write your answer on the faxed document and send it right back.

    - **Over-responding:** Example: if someone asks you for something specific, and you know that by offering more help than was asked for you can prevent the situation or issue from coming back to you in the form of a problem, then isn't it worth it to do more up front? Make a point of over-responding to any situation when there is an opportunity to solve more than one

problem in the process and when you sense that the situation may reappear.

8. **Really listen to others.** When you allow nonrelevant thoughts to intrude into your listening space, you create anxiety for yourself about what you are listening to and what you allow to intrude. You can neither act immediately on the thoughts you allowed to intrude nor can you completely take in what the person with whom you are talking is trying to tell you. You are left feeling incomplete with both.

9. **Decide what you can give up in order to get what you want.** The day has only 24 hours, and yet, how many times have you borrowed from the next day to finish a project and thereby lost valuable sleep, or borrowed from your relationships to pursue a goal, or borrowed from your personal time to work on a project? When we choose among multiple possibilities for how we will spend our time, the universe almost always asks us to choose what we will need to give up. Much pain and suffering resulting from mismanaging time could be avoided if this principle were respected.

10. **Find some time each day for quiet reflection.** When you commit to spending some time each day suspending your thoughts and judgments and creating inner stillness, you'll train your body and mind in what it feels like. With that awareness, you can transform how you experience the flow of time when you are in the world.

Internet Travel Sites Save Time and Money

by Lisa Weber

Reprinted from *Dollars & Cents,* ASAE newsletter, January 2001

Adapted with permission from *The Ultimate Internet Travel Planning Guide,* by Lisa Weber, professional speaker and president of Weber Communications, Tucson, Arizona.

Getting the best travel deals means knowing where to look and reading the fine print. With the Internet, it is easy to make your own travel arrangements, stay in touch while on the road, find directions, and keep your frequent flier miles organized. As a busy working professional, time and money are two of your most important commodities. Using the Web to your advantage, you can be sure not to waste either.

Airline tickets

How can you get the cheapest airline ticket? Getting the best price for an airline ticket takes a little time, but it is well worth it because the savings can be astronomical. Check out these sites first, making sure to write down the fares for comparison:

- Expedia.com,
- Trip.com,
- Lowestfare.com, and
- Cheap Tickets, Inc.

Next, call the airlines, and inquire about their prices. Sometimes the ticket agent can give you a better price than what you've found on the Internet, or vice versa.

Another alternative is to go to one of the name-your-own price sites, such as Priceline.com, reduce the lowest fare by 20 percent, and see what you get. Be aware, however, that once you choose to purchase your tickets from a third-party company, you are usually locked into an agreement if your price is accepted. You'll be notified as such within 24 hours, and if it's at your price, your credit card—which you must provide up front—will be charged. Also, be aware that you cannot choose the time when you fly and that you may not be able to earn frequent flier miles.

When booking airline tickets online, be sure to read the fine print. Most companies charge an additional fee, sometimes up to $75, for any changes.

Keep track of your frequent flier miles online with MaxMiles MileageMiner, or go to Award Traveler, where you can buy and sell frequent flier miles.

Hotel rooms

When you need to book a hotel room, check out Hotel Discounts and Hotel Insider. Both sites advertise rates up to 65 percent off the published price. If you are looking for a no-frills hotel room, check out Roomsaver.com, where you can print out coupons for hotels such as Red Roof Inns and Holiday Inn Express. These coupons can save you from $5 to $10 per night.

Foreign currency

If you're heading out of the country and want information on foreign currency, go to

- Direct FX,
- OANDA Corp., or
- Exchange Rates.

These sites will give you the current exchange rates and allow you to purchase currency online. As with banks, there will be a service fee, and there is usually a fee for overnight delivery.

Car rental

When renting a car, it is best to go directly to the car rental company's Web site. A few of the larger companies include

- Alamo,
- Avis,
- National Car Rental, and
- Thrifty Car Rental.

Editor's note: *To take advantage of ASAE discount rates on car rentals, visit ASAE Services, Inc.'s Business Services Web site.*

E-Postage Efficiencies

Reprinted from

ASSOCIATION

MANAGEMENT,

June 2000

For the association executive running a small office, running to the post office—and waiting in long lines—may quickly become a distant memory. The U.S. Postal Service has given the go-ahead to four private firms to offer postage via the Internet. According to *Forbes* (January 10, 2000), "these upstarts—which let you print postal indicia on envelopes using standard printers, along with USPS-verified address labels—are targeting the 22 million home offices and 7.5 million companies with fewer than 100 employees." Perhaps your small-staff association office should be one of them. (Most electronic postage programs require a personal computer with at least 16 megabytes of RAM and a laser or inkjet printer.)

Postage online, not in line Here's how it works.

- **Install software.** You may download software, order CD-ROMs, or buy software from retail stores. Prices vary among providers; some sell the software while others charge monthly fees.

- **Print postage.** The new postage can be used for first-class, priority, and express-mail service, as well as for parcel post. Like other forms of postage such as meter impressions and stamps, the Information Based Indicia is printed on an envelope in the upper right-hand corner, or on a label for an envelope or package. There's no need for special printers; you can print IBI postage directly from your laser or inkjet printer.

- **Mail it.** You can simply drop mail and packages off at your nearest mailbox— or better yet—many locations offer free pick-up service by USPS.

Multiple benefits

A 24-hour online post office is the most obvious advantage. Here are a few of the other benefits to the new e-postage.

- **Print postage anytime.** Purchased postage is stored online or in a special storage vault that plugs into your computer. You may print on envelopes, labels, or documents using a standard printer. At least one service allows you to access your accumulated postage without the need to remain connected to the Internet.

- **Integrate the program with other software.** Internet postage works with many popular software applications, allowing you to apply postage while you do word processing or create invoices.

- **Verify addresses.** USPS requires that address verification be performed, and the programs include a CD-ROM that contains all deliverable addresses in the United States and validates your addresses to ensure faster delivery of your mail.

Early drawbacks

As with many new technology applications, there have been some reported growing pains. Some of the programs don't yet print labels, some establish a minimum monthly fee even if you don't buy any postage that month, and others have been known to disrupt certain computer operations. Check these things out before selecting a provider.

And, of course, there is a convenience charge for the service, varying from a monthly fee ($15 for one of the services) to a flat fee of 10 percent of postage purchased. Visit the service Web sites for more information.

How to Save Money on Printing

By Margo Vanover Porter

Reprinted from *Association Publishing Directory*, ASSOCIATION MANAGEMENT, November 2001

Why waste a single dollar of your printing budget? That's the philosophy of economy-conscious association executives, who are searching for ways to conserve their association's cash.

"We're keeping printing costs in line in a couple of ways," says Michael Schindel, manager of graphics communications, Society of Automotive Engineers (SAE), Warrendale, Pennsylvania. "We are trying hard to have a totally digital workflow in place for our magazine."

SAE has been making strides in the digital process for about six years. Schindel explains that authors now follow a prescribed template, eliminating much of the need for editors to manipulate text. "This can reduce the number of proofs for a project," he says. "You're streamlining the production process and cycle."

Advertisers also are strongly encouraged to adapt to the digital age. In media kits, SAE emphasizes its preference for portable document format files, instead of film, for all advertisements. "We are accepting a larger percentage of advertising as PDF files," Schindel says. "For the past three years, we have refined and improved our communication to the agencies to say, 'This is what we prefer.' We have our workflow set up in-house so that as the percentage of digital files increases, we won't need to change our process. We're handling film now as the exception."

Get team buy-in

To further refine workflow, the advertising, editorial, and production staffs have examined every step in the magazine process, asking, "Does this step have value? Can we justify this step?" Schindel hopes by year-end to cut four days out of the monthly magazine's cycle. That can only happen, he says, if advertising, editorial, and production work

together as a three-legged stool. "We all need to commit to this," he says. "We need to work together. We need to communicate. We need to do things as simply as possible and not just take shortcuts."

Schindel already is seeing an improvement in the magazine's bottom line. "Our blueline corrections are less than 5 percent because of the discipline that this process instills in the workflow and a commitment by all people on the team that they'll follow the process," he says. "Four years ago, we were probably at 25 percent blueline corrections. [Reducing that to 5 percent] has resulted in tremendous costs savings."

To control printing costs, SAE also is using more print-on-demand delivery of its technical books and papers. "Print on demand follows the digital workflow concept," Schindel explains. "If a customer wants a product and it's already in our database, we can print it and ship it that day. It gives us an economical way to deliver a final product, and we can tailor the initial print run. If we think the market for a book is 300, that's all we print. Then we print on demand anything else."

What else can you do?

Other tips for working with your printer—and saving money in the process—include the following:

Get competitive bids, even if you have a preferred printer. "Shop around," says Eliza R. Selig, communications manager, Hospitality Financial and Technology Professionals, Austin, Texas. "You probably can stick with the printer of your choice, but let your representative know that you have other options, and don't be shy about asking for a better price."

Selig explains that competition among printers in Austin is high, allowing her to get good prices. Although she's concerned about her printing budget, she admits that she doesn't always accept the low bid. "We try to get the best price, but we also consider the service that we receive. Sometimes a project is just so intensive that we need the service…We need to know that the printer will be looking out for us."

Consider a contract, particularly if you find a vendor that is meeting your needs. "If printers don't know if they will ever get your business again, they are reluctant to discount their prices," says Matteo Pederzoli, director of communications and editor/publisher of IBFInsider, The International Association for Document & Information Management Solutions, Alexandria, Virginia. "While you're trying to get the most for your dollars from them, they're trying to get the most for their dollars from you. A contract gives printers something to look forward to."

Connie Helmlinger, periodicals manager, American Nurses Association, Washington, D.C., agrees. In fact, she has in the past signed a three-year contract with her tabloid newspaper's printer and obtained a discount for doing so. "A three-year discount wouldn't work for us now because we're in a state of change," Helmlinger explains. "We may not offer the same product in two years."

Try a lower grade of paper. A few years ago, Helmlinger switched to a lower grade of paper, but she's hesitant to give this step a blanket endorsement. Initially, she feared that members would perceive the paper change as a decrease in the tabloid's quality. To offset that perception, she increased the use of color. "We really haven't gotten any complaints about the lower grade of paper,"

she says. "Because there's four-color on the cover, that's what people see."

Decrease trim size. "Our printer keeps an eye out for ways that we can cut corners," Helmlinger adds. "A few years ago, we trimmed the size of our tabloid newspaper to cut costs. That saved us money because the newspaper fit on a different web."

But what really thrilled Helmlinger was the reaction of members to the makeover. "We've gotten a lot of compliments from our members on the new size. It really looks better."

Respect schedules. Pederzoli doesn't like to pay rush fees or late charges, so he tries to stick to established schedules. But what happens if a printer surprises you with unexpected rush charges? Pederzoli advises taking a firm stance, politely explaining that you must keep within your budget and that you expect to be warned in advance about rush charges.

"Hang tough," he says. "You should have been forewarned."

Establish a relationship with your printer. Pederzoli believes that by building a personal relationship with his printers, he is in a better position to obtain good prices and service. Because he likes to know with whom he is dealing, he often drops by a printer's facilities for a surprise visit and to take a tour. "I really don't believe in the Anglo-Saxon 'business, only business' relationship," Pederzoli says. "I'm Italian. That doesn't mean that the printer and I have to go out for cappuccinos every night, but behind the pen and set of numbers, there's a mind, too."

A Unique Alternative

By Patricia Harris

Reprinted from
ASSOCIATION
MANAGEMENT,
March 2002

Since the National Information Standards Organization (NISO) includes such members as database providers and information networks as well as associations and societies that support the information and content communities, it's not surprising that members expect NISO to embrace digital technology. But with a staff that on a good day hovers around three and a budget of approximately $500,000, it is always a challenge to meet and exceed our members' expectations in the technology arena.

At the time we decided to upgrade our Web site, I knew that it was in need of more than just refreshment—it needed an overhaul. I knew this was not a project we could perform well in-house; however, contracting with a professional Web design firm, with a price tag estimated at $25,000–$50,000, was beyond our budgetary reach. An affordable alternative that worked for us was to contract with the information technology department of an area university. I supplemented the skills of the student selected to work with us by contracting with a Web site firm to critique the site's design and organization as it emerged. It has cost us well under $10,000 to create the new site. Most importantly, we have met our goals in terms of design, expanded content, and functionality.

Although the dirty work has been contracted out, I have learned that all of the staff have to take some ownership of the site—and that starts at the top.

Case Studies and Lessons Learned

Association Reorganization: Keeping Ahead of the Curve

By Fred Webber and Charlie Van Vlack

Reprinted from ASSOCIATION MANAGEMENT, February 2000

Here's a pop quiz for those of you who feel that the very structure of your association is keeping you from serving your members in the most effective way. The key to running a successful association is:

a. exceeding meeting attendance and booth sales at last year's annual meeting.

b. defining and maintaining brand identity.

c. eliminating departments and committees.

d. increasing membership and reducing attrition.

For the Chemical Manufacturers Association (CMA), Arlington, Virginia, the answer is "c." No, we didn't flunk Association 101. We did, however, break some of the rules—and bend others considerably—in the reorganization of our association, which we coined "CMA 2000" and which officially began in January 1998. We took a nontraditional approach to the restructuring, but so far the reorganized CMA, more than a year in place, is passing the test with our members.

"If it ain't broke, why fix it?"

Prior to the reorganization, CMA appeared—at first glance—to be running like a well-oiled machine. One of the oldest and largest trade associations in the country, we had high member satisfaction, a rock-solid reputation, and healthy finances on our side. Our diverse membership accounted for more than 90 percent of chemical production in the United States. We had succeeded in uniting the industry through our Responsible Care initiative, which makes continual improvement in safe manufacturing and handling practices a requirement of CMA membership. While it seemed we were invincible, we found that our past success actually threatened our future. CMA's organization—more than 300 staff and 2,500 member volunteers—had evolved into a sprawling and increasingly complex system of committees, departments, and issue groups. It took too long to come to a consensus on a given issue, and our advocacy suffered from too strong an internal focus. We often required six or more different groups' approvals before moving ahead with an issue—even the most time-sensitive one.

In the meantime, our member companies were changing their organizations as well, and our structure no longer mirrored theirs. Member companies that once had a monolithic view of issues and were organized around fundamental departments much like ours now had multiple business units with individual leaders. The managers of these business units, newly responsible for their own issues, budgets, and support staffs, began to question how their narrower businesses fit into CMA's system. We needed to improve the relevance of our operations to their business strategies and thereby demonstrate the value of their CMA investment. At the same time, we learned a valuable lesson in structure from our members' corporate models, which were organized into individual business units, with each unit accountable for its own business practices and finances. We wanted to run our association like a business.

We spent time in the field with member companies that had recently reorganized themselves. We wanted early buy-in from our key customers on our ideas. This buy-in process extended to our existing committees and our staff.

Finally, it became clear that CMA was not in the best position to achieve our three strategic goals: earning the public's trust, improving CMA's advocacy impact, and creating member value. We were held back by both the cumbersome nature of our organization and the fact that we were not structured in the most effective and efficient way to address the pressing issues facing our industry. CMA was like a large house in which we had lived for many years, accumulating many possessions, and it was time to do a spring cleaning.

Plotting the course

As surely as we decided change was necessary and inevitable, we knew that the senior staff leadership at CMA had to be the drivers of that change. We had witnessed other reorganizations in which the leadership for change was imposed solely by discontented members. We believed we were in the best position to initiate and drive that change. We first worked on developing a partnership with our board officers—four member company leaders of our board of directors—for while we were mitigating the effort, the substance of the new organization had to be driven by a member-staff partnership. We spent time in the field with member companies that had recently reorganized themselves. We wanted early buy-in from our key customers on our ideas. This buy-in process extended to our existing committees and our staff. We wanted everyone to know early that something big was going to happen at CMA, and we wanted them to be an integral part of the process.

We knew we needed a ground-up review of our structure and processes, but we needed help getting there—specifically, the help of two different consultants. Why two? We deliberately planned to have a break between phases of the reorganization in order to keep control of the project firmly in our own hands, and not those of a consulting firm. We wanted to drive the change and to have the consultants facilitate it.

The research phase. For the first part of the reorganization, we deliberately hired an outside-the-Beltway consultant who did not specialize in associations: James Miller

and Company of Houston. Jim Miller was in a good position to analyze our operations and compare them to a corporate example, which was our model. Hiring a "business" consultant, we believed, would send a strong message to our members that this would not be a typical association reorganization.

Miller's work involved two phases of research. Initially, the company conducted approximately 50 interviews with staff and individual members, determining what was working well at CMA and what areas could use improvement. Next, more than 200 staff and members were enlisted as part of an indepth analysis of CMA's operating systems. During this part of the reorganization, all aspects of CMA were put on the proverbial table for examination, and nothing was spared.

We found that although the current system had served CMA well through the years—especially in sharing information, involving members, and developing resources—we spent too much time talking among ourselves and not enough time talking to members of Congress, state agencies, international organizations, regulatory agencies, and other key public organizations and stakeholders. We needed a structure that kept the strong points that had become the hallmark of CMA, yet allowed us to move more quickly and effectively in our external relations.

Issue and program teams. Miller's hard-edged analysis helped us conceive of such an organization—the backbone of today's CMA 2000. Instead of being organized around disciplinary departments—such as communication, state affairs, and the like—the new operating system comprised issue and program teams made up of members and staff from various disciplines, devoted to particular issues such as public health and market access.

The issue and program teams are supported by what we call shared services, made up of CMA staff, which can provide additional functional support to an issue team when needed. We also have corporate service groups that handle the daily operations of

CMA (such as accounting and human resources) that affect the entire organization.

By January 1998, the first phase of analysis and conceptual design was complete. Miller's findings and our preliminary design concepts were presented to CMA's board of directors, who gave us the go-ahead for the next phase of the reorganization.

"There's no way you're going to pull this off."

For the next phase, we hired a consultant well known to us, Mike Tate of Tate-Francesca Company, Arlington, Virginia. We knew that Tate, who was familiar with associations and CMA in particular, would understand what it would take to help build out the conceptual design. At the same time, Tate was objective, helped keep us on track, and constantly challenged us and kept us from backsliding into the "old CMA" way of doing things.

It was a defining moment in CMA's history when the board unanimously approved the design and budget of CMA 2000.

We set an aggressive timetable for putting the new design and budget in place—a mere three months. People outside the organization kept telling us that we would never be able to complete the work within the given time. With determination, we were able to prove them wrong.

From February to April 1998, the "design groups"—composed of both members and staff—worked at breakneck speed. Design groups were formed in several areas: member relations, issue and program management, external relations, information technology, human resources, business processes, and internal communication. While we asked some staff to make the new design work their first priority, others were asked to keep "CMA '98" on track—the "regular" work of the association being just as important an endeavor. We committed to the board that we would complete the design while still delivering on our program and issue priorities.

Creating business plans. Given a draft mission statement and some basic guidelines to work with, each design team was asked to write a business plan for the new team or shared service. The design groups were given the tasks of describing expected deliverables and milestones; identifying operating elements, including how and when processes should be done; establishing a business case for change; and defining key connection points to be made between groups. It took long hours and infinite patience from the members and staff, but we managed to deliver the overall framework of the new CMA, as well as the operating plans for each team and shared service, by our deadline.

The result is a completely new CMA, with more than 70 percent of the staff organized into issue and program teams that concentrate our resources on achieving specific goals. These teams are CMA's primary mechanism for issue advocacy and program delivery. The rest of the staff supports the issue and program teams. CMA's corporate services—executive services, human resources, information management and technology, member relations, finance, and legal—ensure that CMA can function as an organization. Shared services teams—such as external relations and state affairs—help provide necessary "surge" support to the teams.

New partnerships. Each of the issue and program teams has co-leaders, one from the membership and one from the CMA staff. The makeup of each team also reflects the new partnership between members and staff as they work together on a given issue. Members who belong to teams are selected based on their varied skills and experience with the issue. In selecting staff members for teams, we followed the same philosophy: fitting the right people in the right jobs. Depending on a team's particular needs, we staffed each team with federal, state, and international advocates; lawyers; communication professionals; and issue/policy specialists. Each team has a unique mix of skills and talents—unlike our old committees that may have had only one kind of professional (e.g., all environmental specialists).

The result has been a cohesive group working on each issue we choose to tackle.

For instance, instead of having to wait for a press release written by the communication department, a team can use its own communication specialist, saving time while also benefiting from the fact that someone most familiar with the subject matter is doing the writing. Of course, for those projects that require more resources or affect CMA at large, teams can turn to CMA's shared services, which can provide additional "flex" to meet peak demands.

We felt it was also crucial to maintain and cultivate outside groups who could advise the teams and thus improve our advocacy. We therefore set up what we call roundtables for our four key venues: state, federal legislative, federal regulatory, and international. These roundtables are made up of member company representatives and staff who work on fostering external relationships, counseling teams on strategy, and representing CMA to policy makers. These groups ensure coordination among the teams as we deliver our advocacy and provide the foundation for our long-term success in each of these venues.

Member services center. We wanted to make customer service one of our hallmarks. We created a member services center, which is designed to offer members "one-stop shopping" for their initial CMA questions. Staffed by four employees who are specifically trained to answer members' questions, the member services center is designed to handle everything from meeting registration to publications fulfillment to answering questions about general issues. For a member who has a concern that cannot be responded to immediately, the member services center will either find out the answer or put the member in touch with the appropriate CMA staff member on one of the teams.

Hiring executives from the industry

Taking member relations a step closer to our members—actually, to their doors—is another important element of CMA 2000. We have accomplished this goal through our four member relations executives (MREs),

former senior executives from the industry we hired to work in the field. Unique in the association field, the MREs have an average of 25 years of experience in our industry. They speak the same language as our members and enjoy instant credibility with them. Each MRE is responsible for a region of the United States, traveling to our members' facilities, learning more about our members' needs, and communicating the value CMA provides. We felt it was crucial to have increased face-to-face interaction with our member companies at their facilities to stay in close and constant touch with a broader range of our members than would ever travel to Washington, D.C. Currently, they are in the process of profiling each member so that we know each of their businesses, what their interests are, and what resources they uniquely can bring to bear on our program and issue teams. The four MREs are also on-hand to take care of members' specific needs—adding a personal dimension to our customer service.

Creating member networks

We also needed ways in which to get regular feedback and involvement from the members, filling the gap left by our committees, which the board gave us permission to disband when we originally presented the plan for CMA 2000. Importantly, we wanted to keep the parts of CMA that the members most valued—the networking and information—while eliminating the burden of always having to travel to Washington, D.C. The solution was creating member networks—larger groups of individual members who could communicate about a given issue with the organization and with each other. Networks have been established in more than 20 areas. The network system is designed to improve CMA's advocacy clout as well as encourage peer interaction. Networks operate through our members-only extranet site and face-to-face meetings, driven by member demand. Some networks are directly aligned with teams, which decide the frequency of their meetings; others form on their own when members decide that an issue warrants a group gathering. In either case, all network meetings are designed to be break even, keeping in line with one of the goals of CMA 2000—to transfer many of our internally focused expenditures to external actions.

Another aspect of our new structure is the issue review team, which primarily assists in setting priorities and allocating resources for teams. The issue review team, which comprises senior member company representatives and CMA staff, makes recommendations to the board and CMA's finance and executive committees. Members who serve on the team represent a diverse mix: environmental health and safety professionals, lobbyists, communication professionals, and notably, a CEO and three business unit managers, who provide a unique corporate outlook. Using an advocacy scoring model developed by CMA, the team evaluates the advocacy potential and resource requirements for prospective issues. CMA's executive committee pursues or drops individual issues, based on the team's recommendations.

In April, we presented to the board the CMA 2000 design and the new budget to support it. It was a defining moment in CMA's history when the board unanimously approved the design and budget of CMA 2000. It was important for us to remember that we started CMA 2000 to become both a more effective and a more efficient organization. Our new budget reflected these twin goals. While the number of CMA staff members was reduced, the budget did not fluctuate much due to the specialized positions we created. What did change was the accountability for budgets, which now rests in the hands of the individual teams. Once the finance committee recommends our budget and the board approves it, the board considers the implementation of the budget a management authority.

We moved quickly from the final design to building the new CMA. By the end of May 1998, only five months after the board approved our initial concepts, and fewer than six weeks after approval of the final design and budget, CMA staff were informed of their team assignments. Within another month, they had begun work on their new teams. Staffing reorganization was necessarily as substantial as our structural reconfiguration, which we couldn't have implemented without parallel staffing changes.

The human element

Of course, having the proper structure in place is only one part of the equation. In order for things to add up properly, we needed to fill the association with the right people. We had to face the fact that not all of our staff fit into the new CMA. We had accumulated many mid-level generalists, and in most cases, what we needed were more senior specialists. We initiated a hiring freeze while the design was in progress to achieve maximum flexibility in filling our new team and shared service positions.

We started with a clean slate. In essence, we let go the entire staff and offered them the opportunity to apply for one or more of the newly created positions. Our human resources staff developed and implemented a competency-based measurement system so that CMA's staff would be focused on core competencies. Using this tool, we evaluated the applicants according to how they scored in each of these competencies, including how well they would work in a team environment and how receptive they would be to change.

We offered early retirement for qualifying employees. In some cases, we had to make the hard decision to involuntarily separate others who did not match our needs. We offered these individuals good separation packages and job counseling. By the end of the initial phase of the reorganization, there was a staff turnover of approximately 30 percent, including 26 positions that were eliminated entirely.

We also felt that CMA needed an infusion of new blood and energy. To obtain that, we hired some people from outside of our industry. It took us more than eight months to fill all the vacancies, but in the end we believed it was worth the extra time to get the right people.

One of the most unconventional human resources changes we made was hiring a CMA communication professional—who for years had developed media messages and written speeches for executives and board members—to head up our information management and technology area. We wanted someone in this position who was a true expert at managing information—and translating the technology into manageable content. A key design element of CMA 2000 was to achieve state-of-the-art technology and the technical expertise to support it. However, we felt it was less important to get a person who could understand the "gigabyte" side of information technology than it was to place one of our best communicators in the leadership role to use the technology to link our members, reach our external stakeholders, and communicate our positions.

Measuring performance

One of our goals in the reorganization was to stay nimble and be flexible with changing times and circumstances. To do so, we must constantly evaluate ourselves with a new CMA 2000 yardstick. The measurement tools have changed.

We have moved toward a 360-degree review in which all team members (members and staff) participate. Staff are evaluated by not only their supervisors but also by those who work for them, as well as, in some cases, members who are in a position to appraise their work. In addition to individual evaluations, the issue review team will evaluate teams on how they have met their performance goals detailed in their business plans. Staff will be evaluated on their team performance as well as on their individual performance.

Aside from our human resources measurements, we have adopted the "Balanced Scorecard"—which focuses on financial performance, customer knowledge, internal business processes, and learning and growth—to evaluate team and shared service performance. How knowledgeable and up-to-date is our staff? To what degree do our internal business processes support our mis-

sions? How satisfied are our members? How healthy are our financial reports? In some cases, we don't know the answers to these questions yet.

We do know the success and speed with which we have been able to move forward on a number of key issues since the reorganization. At the old CMA, we had to work on an issue with our efforts dispersed throughout the organization, with different departments working on different parts of the issue. Now, each team is directly accountable and has the resources it needs, and is able to progress more quickly and to attack issues head-on. For instance, within a short period of time, we were able to launch a voluntary testing program for more than 2,800 high-production-volume chemicals, and we are establishing consortia to sponsor the testing in a cost-efficient manner for our members. In another example, CMA's distribution team is addressing the issue of rail competitiveness, using its member network to contact Congress, conduct a survey of rail service problems, and improve CMA's advocacy. In the old CMA, both of these efforts would have been hindered by multiple clearances and checkpoints, competition for resources among the departments, and the inability to move quickly enough to have the needed impact on legislative and regulatory affairs.

Speed bumps

We have had some early successes, but we are still fine-tuning our efforts. The work of CMA 2000 did not stop with the overall design—we are constantly looking to be better. The member networks, for instance, while a crucial element of CMA's new structure, are one of the least understood elements of the association. We are launching a new campaign to reintroduce the members to the advantages of networks, and hope to bolster their participation in this valuable association resource. We found that our members associate the concept of a network with computers only, and we need to assure them that member networks offer face-to-face meetings as well as instant electronic access and research tools. We want to be sure that all members feel they have a voice within a network—whether their participation is via electronic means or in person.

The networks illustrate that we have a long way to go in certain areas, and our Web site and members-only extranet site were no exceptions. The members-only site offered vast resources of up-to-date information, but we had not engaged enough members to take advantage of this tool. We have relaunched the site, giving it a user-friendly name, "MemberExchange" (we had a staff contest to name the site), and organized the content in a more usable format.

We met with some resistance when we scrapped our committee structure in favor of member-staff teams. Since the number of member slots available on the teams was much smaller than the number of members serving on the committees, some ex-committee members were disgruntled and felt there was no longer a place for their input. Although we have not resolved this issue totally, we are trying our best to encourage ex-committee members—and all members, for that matter—to participate in the member networks.

Believe it or not, we received complaints for moving too quickly on some issues. Although the multiple layers and clearances in the old CMA sometimes slowed operations down to the point of ineffectiveness, the swiftness of the streamlined CMA 2000 upset others who were comfortable with the old pace. The chemical testing program is one good example: Although we were proud of our ability to respond quickly and initiate a program that could potentially save our association members millions of dollars, some members felt that they were not given enough time to provide input before the decision was made. We are doing our best to keep the membership duly informed, yet want them to know that the organization has changed to become more nimble and quick.

Would we do it again? In a heartbeat. However, there would be a few things we would do differently. For instance, we would avoid the hassle of preparing two separate budgets. Since our CMA 2000 work was concurrent with our normal budget development, our original plan was to develop a "placeholder" budget for our last fiscal year while we worked on the association redesign. We believed that once the CMA 2000 plan was approved, we would then reconfigure the budget. Our finance committee had other ideas, and in March asked us to redesign not only the association, but the association's budget as well—with both deliverables due in fewer than four weeks. Although we may have been able to avoid the additional workload by communicating with the finance committee earlier, this setback was a minor one.

The transition into CMA 2000, while not seamless, has been well worth the hard work. We are proud of the successes CMA 2000 has fostered in recent months. We have an excited, motivated staff and members who are responding to the new energy CMA 2000 is creating. Now we are in the habit of looking ahead, challenging ourselves rather than maintaining status quo. Our goal is to maintain this foresight and to keep looking for ways in which to serve our members better.

Change Innovations

These actions were instrumental in the success of our reorganization:

- Improved relevance of operations to members' business strategies.
- Spent time with member companies that had reorganized themselves.
- Planned for a break between phases of the reorganization in order to retain control.
- Shifted to an external focus.
- Planned new organizational structure.
- Put business plans at the heart of the project.
- Created a staff-volunteer partnership.
- Set up advisory roundtables.
- Created a member services center.
- Assigned member relations executives to different regions to communicate with members.

- Eliminated committees.
- Fired staff and invited them to re-apply.
- Hired a communication professional to manage information and technology.
- Initiated all-staff performance review.
- Adopted "balanced scorecard" as measurement tool.

Keeping Communication Flowing

by Fred Webber and Charlie Van Vlack

Reprinted from ASSOCIATION MANAGEMENT, February 2000

Early on during the reorganization, CMA began an all-out communication campaign to several key audiences: members; staff; and other stakeholders, including coalitions, associations, key contractor and supplier companies, and the trade press. We communicated to our membership through traditional vehicles, such as our membership magazine and our weekly electronic newsletter. We also held regular, informal briefings for groups of members visiting our headquarters, and took the show on the road whenever there was an opportunity.

The staff received frequent e-mails from us, detailing each step of the process. We also held occasional brown bag lunches to give the staff insight into different aspects of the reorganization. Periodically, we held town hall meetings in which the staff could ask questions and air concerns. We developed a "CMA 2000 Communication Room" where staff could post questions anonymously on our internal e-mail system. We also devised an electronic bulletin board as part of the communication effort so that staff would have easy access to information.

Some tips for keeping the lines of communication open during a major reorganization:

- **Communicate early and often.** For staff members, internal e-mail updates are an excellent way to get the word out and make them understand that senior management has not forgotten about them. Walk around and let the staff ask you personally about what direction the association is taking—and let them give you their ideas about possible directions. For members, try a variety of media, since different members read different publications. Regular updates on the association Web site and in the member magazine, perhaps via a regular column, will ensure that members do not feel left in the dark.

- **Ask for input and help.** If members and staff feel they can make a difference in the reorganization process, they are more likely to support it. If you get early input from your stakeholders, the resulting reorganization is more likely to be successful because the change comes from within rather than from the top.

- **Acknowledge the downside.** With every reorganization, there are sacrifices to be made, and it's best not to sugarcoat them. Win the respect of your stakeholders by being straightforward about the side effects of the reorganization—which could include challenging demands and changes for the staff, the difficulty of adapting to a new style of work, or the start-up time required for new member groups. Make sure that every process enacted is transparent and that you have nothing to hide.

- **Emphasize the positive.** While there may be temporary setbacks during any reorganization, they will be outweighed by benefits reaped in the future. Remind your stakeholders that the long-term prospects are bright indeed—whether they are increased opportunities and responsibilities for your staff or more effective lobbying for your members. At CMA we actually experienced less staff turnover immediately after the reorganization was announced than at any other time of the year because employees were interested and excited to find their niche in the new CMA.

Reprinted from
Executive IdeaLink,
ASAE newsletter,
March 2001

Association Turnaround: Interview With Barbara Byrd Keenan, CAE

It was 1990. The Community Associations Institute (CAI), Alexandria, Virginia, had a deficit fund balance. Its membership was in decline, and there were no reserves. Worse, an unsuccessful computer conversion put financial and membership records in disarray. Dues invoices couldn't be printed, CAI couldn't pay its bills, and staff was unmotivated and undisciplined, making basic daily operations almost impossible. CAI was in jeopardy of locking its doors.

The CAI board, executive committee, and key volunteer leaders thought (hoped) a turnaround might be possible. They hired Barbara Byrd Keenan, CAE, then executive vice president of the International Association of Hospitality Accountants, Austin, Texas, to take over as EVP of CAI.

The turnaround

Executive IdeaLink: What motivated you to take on the challenge of an association in crisis?

Barbara Byrd Keenan, CAE: The ability to demonstrate my skills and position myself for further career advancement. I had the full support of volunteer leaders, and CAI was primed for unlimited growth in programs and services.

Executive IdeaLink: How did you establish your relationship with the board of directors?

Keenan: I insisted on and received solid, unqualified commitment to do whatever it took to turn CAI around. I was lucky. I had never met members or volunteer leaders as devoted to an organization as the CAI board. One of the board members managed the books off-site for the first month, and other leaders worked on CAI business from their offices. Communication was con-

stant—I talked to the top volunteers at least once a day for months.

Executive IdeaLink: What was your strategy for managing member relationships?

Keenan: I literally walked into a stack of hate mail. Our first step was to acknowledge the obvious—we were doing poorly in terms of member service. I answered as many letters as I could, and I didn't promise anything that CAI could not deliver. I tried to be realistic about what CAI could accomplish and gave relatively low expectations to members at first.

Executive IdeaLink: What was the number one challenge related to staffing, and what was your strategy for overcoming that challenge?

Keenan: The biggest obstacle was putting staff in place who not only had the skills to do the job, but were also people who became energized by high-risk, high-reward situations. I let a lot of staff members go. I was forced to make a quick, yet thoughtful, assessment of skills and motivation. With those whom I hired, I was very clear and honest about the state of things at CAI, but I also painted a vision of what I thought was possible for the future.

Executive IdeaLink: What did your first year as executive vice president look like?

Keenan: That first year was a long one. I, along with other key staff, worked 12-hour days plus half days on weekends. Communication with staff, volunteer leaders, and members was constant. It was important to help them keep sight of the big picture while making improvements that set the stage to act strategically.

I spoke daily with the chief elected officer and treasurer so that we could constantly refocus and reposition. I held full staff meetings every three to four weeks to keep staff up to date and to indoctrinate new staff members. A monthly newsletter to members and chapters kept them informed of the many changes at CAI during that year. I think I was "positively impatient" that first year. I wanted things to happen quickly, but I tried to stay optimistic when CAI endured the inevitable time delays.

Executive IdeaLink: What were your three primary strategic goals?

Keenan: Stabilizing financial operations and cash flow; refocusing revenue-producing programs, especially education; and introducing comprehensive strategic planning once operations were stable.

This plan progressed in several stages. The basic phase was completed in approximately 18 months at which time a strategic plan was in place.

Executive IdeaLink: What's your best advice to fellow nonprofit/association CEOs tackling a similar challenge?

Keenan:

- Insist on unwavering support from top volunteer leaders.
- Be very clear with short- and long-term goals. Plan in phases and be relentless on objectives.
- Walk your talk on customer service. Become the epitome of excellence on member and customer service.
- Be the keeper of the flame and protector of the vision. Don't let staff see your fear, and communicate the enormity of issues to staff in manageable pieces.
- Make informed, thoughtful, yet speedy decisions. There's no time for careful analysis of everything, so decisions must be based on less than perfect information.
- Be a multitasker. Work simultaneously on financial issues, member services, computer concerns, the organization's most profitable programs, and more.
- Build a strong staff team. You need people who get energized by building.
- Be patient, especially when you know you can't do or fix everything at once.

- Balance doing with listening. Be the lightening rod of information by taking the time to listen to staff and members.
- Shift from strategic to tactical mode once you're above water.
- Celebrate increments of success. Catch folks doing things right and give them praise.
- Keep your sense of humor. This is most important.

Today

CAI is thriving thanks to a dedicated staff, keen leadership, and continuing efforts by Keenan, now president of CAI. During her tenure, CAI implemented numerous educational and certification programs for associations, community managers, and attorneys in the industry and launched federal and state legislative and advocacy programs. In addition, the organization has grown its membership by 65 percent; built substantial reserves; and been recognized by the association industry many times for excellence in educational programming, marketing, publications, graphic and Web design, and government affairs.

CAI: Yesterday and Today

	1990	2000
Annual Budget	$3.2 million	$7.6 million
Membership	10,000	16,500
Destination Programs	2	6
Education Programs	43 courses; 2 law seminars; 2 national conferences	117 courses; 2 law seminars; 2 national conferences
Association Awards	0	15

Reprinted from
Dollars & Cents,
ASAE newsletter,
March 2000

Innovative Partnership Revives an Association

By Brenda Luper, CPA

The National Association of the Remodeling Industry, Alexandria, Virginia, won a trophy in ASAE's 1999 Awards of Excellence in Finance and Administration.

In March 1998, the National Association of the Remodeling Industry (NARI) was in fiscal trouble. The association was holding its annual trade show and convention in Chicago and was experiencing a steep two-year decline in trade show net revenues. In the past, the profits from the trade show had almost equaled NARI's annual dues revenues. And the drop in revenue was seriously affecting the association's viability. Exhibitors and other members were deeply concerned about recent less-than-favorable trade show experiences and the future of the event.

Concurrently, NARI was searching for a new executive vice president (EVP), the association's top staff position. A leading candidate was asked to critique the trade show and conference. After presenting his recommendations to the board, he was hired, and within a week he met with the elected president to prepare an emergency budget proposal. The proposal took into account the severe revenue decline and suggested heavy cutbacks in expenditures. In light of future-revenue overestimates from a variety of sources—figures prepared by a previous round of staff and budget task force members—budgets were slashed.

A crisis budget

The new budget was presented to the board at its mid-June 1998 meeting. The meeting began with an atmosphere of suspicion and denial, but by the end of the meeting the board had approved the contingency plan and accepted most of the cutbacks.

It was clear, however, that dramatic reductions alone were not the solution. Eventually the budget cuts would erode membership programs and services and end in a downward revenue spiral.

In addition, the board was divided in its assessment of NARI's future viability. Some board members saw only doom and gloom, while others believed that revenues would reach their former heights at the next trade show and convention in March 1999.

However, by the fall of 1998, it was obvious that the target revenue goals and trade show sales were not being met.

Exploring options

By November 1998, the executive committee authorized exploring other revenue alternatives, but the diversity of approaches indicated that the next board meeting would not be pleasant. The suggestions included:

- selling the trade show;
- acquiring another trade show;
- obtaining an investor partner;
- joining forces with another association's or publisher's trade show; and
- expanding the trade show to other trade types and specialties.

The fiscal crisis continued to deepen. By December 1998 it was obvious that the trade show was not going to meet its revenue objectives, but the sensitive situation had to be kept quiet, as it could result in exhibitor cancellations. That would not only lead to further losses—a projected net shortfall of more than $350,000 on a $2 million budget—but also would likely cripple on-site sales of exhibit space for the 2000 show.

Despite the slowdown in exhibit sales, the EVP and staff met to devise expanded marketing plans to draw more participants. NARI was determined to put every effort into creating an atmosphere of success around the show. The association substantially increased the marketing of the trade show, including direct mail, radio announcements, cooperative advertising arrangements, and a new Web site.

In the meantime, an emergency meeting of the budget task force was called, and its members undertook serious deficit planning. By the end of January 1999, it was clear that without intervention the association would be in Chapter 11 reorganization, with its reserves gone and cash exhausted, before October 1999. The clear option now was a partnership with another organization or an investor.

An innovative partnership

In an innovative partnership arrangement with an industry partner, NARI avoided going into Chapter 11 and now is a viable entity. The agreement provided several key benefits.

- The trade show rights were sold to an industry partner in a partnership arrangement that will last for 10 years.
- The association will not lose its identity with the trade show, and NARI's name will remain associated with the show, thus avoiding a member revolt that was in the offing.
- The sale of the trade show provided an immediate and much-needed influx of cash and generated $.5 million, equivalent to twice the average net earnings of the show during the previous two years.
- Future revenue streams from the industry partner included $.4 million during fall 1999. The total sales price, paid across six years (1999–2005) in guaranteed payments, will be several million dollars, more than the net earnings of

the trade show across the previous six years.

The new partnership was announced before the March 1999 trade show, reinvigorating the trade show exhibitors and sending a positive signal about future shows. On-site sales for the next year began to take off.

Additionally, in July 1999, NARI signed an agreement for a new venture with a major Internet company. This agreement added approximately $100,000 minimum in net revenues each year for the next seven years, plus other earnings potential.

A new focus

At the July 1999 board meeting, due to these new successful partnerships, NARI was able to plan new projects and programs. Chapter services and programs had been at a minimum for several years, but the influx of money allowed a series of programs and membership efforts to be undertaken. These include a new certification program, expanded educational programming at the regional level, new insurance programs, enhanced Web site offerings, and much-needed servicing of local chapters, demonstrating a commitment to the new strategic plan.

The partnership arrangement allowed NARI to refocus its staff and volunteer efforts from exhibit sales and trade show management to professional development for members. With new revenue in place, staff cutbacks ended. Staff with skills and experience that matched the new strategic plan were hired.

The board and its committees are now invigorated with new purpose and with the necessary resources to accomplish the association's long-term objectives and to fully service the needs of its members.

Reprinted from
ASSOCIATION
MANAGEMENT,
August 2001

Reinvention Results: How One Small Association Generated the Buy-in to Broaden Its Scope

By Paul W. Rankin

I t all began on a flight to Thailand.

En route to the annual meeting of our international confederation, I sat next to Bill Shocklee, the newly elected chief elected officer of the Association of Container Reconditioners (ACR), Landover, Maryland. Our conversation began innocently enough: Bill wanted my views on the likely effect that a series of recently proposed mergers involving member companies would have on the association's bottom line.

As the founder and CEO of a rapidly growing industrial container reconditioning company in St. Louis, Bill had a reputation as a clear-thinking, no-nonsense entrepreneur. I knew he wanted a succinct assessment of our current situation, several options for the future, and my recommendation on the best course of action.

Having briefly discussed some of these issues with Bill at an orientation meeting, I knew to be prepared with the facts. I told him our 56-year-old association—with a staff of four and annual operating budget of $700,000—was facing a critical period. During the past four years, membership had decreased by 15 percent from its peak, when we had approximately 113 voting and an additional 50 supplier and associate members. Most of the losses came from our "middle class"—the mid-sized companies that accounted for about 20 percent of the total membership. Mergers and acquisitions were occurring regularly, and we could expect more in the coming months. Family-owned businesses, once a clear majority of the membership, were poised to lose their majority status.

The forces behind the trends

What was driving these changes in our industry?

- **Member companies were rapidly expanding their business portfolios to include a variety of industrial packagings.** For example, 10 years earlier, 95 percent of association members were engaged exclusively in the business of steel drum reconditioning. Now, 80 percent of the members were handling other container types in addition to steel drums. This change had come about because two alternate container types—plastic drums and intermediate bulk containers (which in 1990 represented only about 20 percent of the industrial packaging market measured by capacity)—had increased market share to about 40 percent by 1996. We anticipated these market trends would continue, although at a somewhat less robust pace.

- **The business of supplying industrial packagings was evolving rapidly.** For many years the lines of demarcation separating manufacturers from reconditioners were clear. That was no longer the case. Several manufacturers had purchased or were preparing to purchase reconditioning operations, and some reconditioners were creating strategic business alliances with one or more manufacturers.

- **A growing number of reconditioning companies were transitioning away from a local or regional service orientation.** Instead, they were becoming transregional or national in scope.

• Our association's finances, always dependent on member dues for approximately 80 percent of total revenue, were beginning to suffer despite a recent dues increase. In addition, meeting attendance and publication sales were trending downward, a pattern likely to continue and possibly accelerate as more buyouts took place.

Despite these trends, ACR was not facing an immediate financial crisis. The group still represented about 90 percent of the industry (measured by production capacity). And it was the only organization of its kind in the United States. However, as the influence of family-owned businesses waned, and as fewer and larger companies paid a greater share of total dues, we presumed that support for dues increases would be increasingly difficult to obtain.

How the planning process worked

Bill and I agreed on three things. First, the association had to broaden its membership base to ensure a reliable revenue stream. Second, a merger wasn't viable. When one such effort had been attempted two years earlier, the result had been a costly and time-consuming failure. Finally, we had to consider every other possibility for restructuring—no matter how far-reaching the changes might be. We followed these four steps to help us plan our future direction.

1. **Create a representative planning committee.** Our planning committee included our elected officers, several highly respected elder statesmen, our general counsel, and a few younger members who were emerging leaders in the group. In addition, we took into account geographic representation, company size, and professional expertise (e.g., finance). The committee members, mostly company CEOs, all had the vision and creativity to act boldly.

2. **Write a summary document and set the stage for change.** Before our first committee meeting, each member received a memorandum summarizing discussions to date and a description of the financial, membership, and organizational issues facing the association.

At its first meeting, the committee concluded that incremental change would be no more helpful than a fad diet; things might appear different for a while, but in no time we'd be looking for fixes to the same old problems. Therefore, we decided to propose revolutionary changes in the organization and management structure of our association.

3. **Assign research.** Members of the committee appointed me to develop a white paper. This research paper used ideas derived from their brainstorming sessions as well as input from other sources, including ASAE and other association executives with whom I conferred.

4. **Make recommendations.** As requested, the suggestions were revolutionary. My white paper concluded that "an opportunity exists to bring under one roof firms that recondition, manufacture, distribute, and recycle" industrial packagings. By expanding the group to include manufacturers, the association would still serve its core constituency—steel drum reconditioners. But we would open a path to growth and prosperity by embracing the entire nonbulk and intermediate bulk packaging spectrum.

Broadening our scope meant two things: The association would have to change its name to reflect its new membership, and we would have to allow manufacturers to participate as full members. This meant giving them the right to vote and serve on the board of directors.

The paper also suggested that ACR's half-century-old regional structure should be eliminated. Instead, it should be reorganized along product lines: steel drum, plastic drum, and intermediate bulk container.

Each of these divisions, which came to be called product groups, would be largely self-governing and composed of manufacturers, distributors, and reconditioners of the various products.

Building much-needed consensus

The white paper served as a springboard for discussion. Members of the planning committee met four times in 45 days, twice in person and twice by conference call. Before each session we made sure that everyone had the minutes of the previous meeting and that the white paper was revised to reflect current thinking.

The planning committee decided to present its ideas to the board of directors at the association's spring meeting. Because this was such a critical point in the process, careful preparation was vital. Our staff compiled a lengthy memorandum explaining the issues and distributed it to every board and executive committee member approximately two weeks before the meeting. Bill and I also called each board member to discuss the proposals and ascertain if any serious opposition to the concept was forming.

Bill and a well-respected planning committee member presented the proposal, being careful to include a detailed discussion of the group's current and projected financial and membership status. Not surprisingly, the board discussed the matter at length. But in the end, Bill sought, and received, unanimous consent to move forward with the planning process.

Knowing that we had general board support, the planning committee members accelerated their schedule. Working primarily by e-mail and conference calls, they established strict timetables for developing a draft governance memorandum (e.g., mission statement, administrative structures) and consequential bylaws amendments.

Throughout this phase, Bill and I agreed to speak every day. Both of us believe in the value of personal discussion. E-mail and fax are excellent ways to transmit information, but crucial subtleties like tentativeness and

doubt get lost on screen and on paper. If the reorganization was to succeed, we had to be absolutely certain, all the time, about where we both stood on every issue.

Because our association had such a small staff—only four—this planning process meant a great deal of extra work, particularly paperwork. We decided to spread the load and make it a team effort. The two people most intimately involved in the process, other than myself, were my office manager/bookkeeper, who created and revised financial statements and membership assessments; and my administrative assistant, who prepared our graphs and charts. My view is that by keeping everyone involved in the process, concerns about the effects of possible changes were held to a minimum. This also helped staff buy in to the process, a fact that was crucial to the success of this effort.

Pursuing the final approval

By July, only five months after our first formal discussion about expansion, the planning committee completed a fully elaborated draft governance memorandum as well as a set of draft bylaws for the proposed new organization. The governance memorandum included

- a new name, mission statement, and guiding principles;
- a completely reconfigured organizational structure;
- revised election procedures;
- recommendations regarding dues and finance issues; and
- an implementation timetable.

Approximately two weeks before our summer board meeting, we distributed all this material to the board of directors, the executive committee, and a number of the association's old hands. During the interim period, we asked each planning committee member to contact several board members personally to discuss the proposals and answer questions.

Once again, Bill and I called every member of the board prior to the meeting.

The committee met by conference call before the board meeting to discuss member comments, make needed revisions to the proposal, and outline a game plan for the board meeting. The committee selected an articulate speaker to make the presentation to the board and requested that it be done using PowerPoint, with handouts for all members and observers.

Chairman Shocklee set aside 90 minutes at the board meeting for the presentation and discussion. We knew from our phone calls that support was strong, but we were hoping to gain unanimous approval.

The presentation went well: brief, to the point, but with no relevant detail left out. The most controversial issue—allowing new manufacturers the right to vote and serve on the board—generated some heated remarks from a few of the association's elder statesmen. But they eventually realized that change was essential to the association's long-term survival. The board recommended several revisions to the proposal, all of which the planning committee agreed to.

The 21-member board then approved, with just one dissenting vote, a motion to adopt "...the planning committee proposal...to restructure ACR and establish the Reusable Industrial Packaging Association."

Using the same open-information strategy, we revised the governance plan and drafted bylaws in accordance with board recommendations. Then we distributed them to all of our members 45 days before the annual meeting. A detailed presentation of the plan took place at the general membership meeting. After discussion, the members approved it without a dissenting vote.

Our major success factors

Today, two years after the change, the Reusable Industrial Packaging Association is thriving.

Members believe the new structure has made us stronger and more effective. Although mergers and consolidations have in fact whittled away at our membership base, the product-group structure has attracted many new members. Income from dues is a bit higher than it was two years ago; income from publications and meetings is still declining slowly. But manufacturers have become an integral part of the organization. In fact, several manufacturer representatives serve on our board and executive committee.

I attribute the speed with which our changes took place to two main factors: One was Bill Shocklee's will to move forward. He recognized fully and early the need to expand the scope of our membership base and create a more inclusive operating structure.

Second, the board and membership trusted me to make sound decisions. When this process began, I had been president for eight years, during which time I got to know every single member and visited more than 40 member plants. In addition, I worked hard to make all administrative decisions in as transparent a manner as possible. Many minor decisions that could have turned contentious were handled "behind the curtain"—thus enabling the process to move forward rapidly.

Trust among the board, the membership, and the executive is a prerequisite to any restructuring effort. Looking back, I would not do anything differently.

Reprinted from

Dollars & Cents,

ASAE newsletter,

March 2000

Improved Resource Management Guides a Financial Turnaround

By Brenda Luper, CPA

The Jacksonville Chamber of Commerce, Florida, won a certificate of achievement in ASAE's 1999 Awards of Excellence in Finance and Administration.

The Jacksonville Chamber of Commerce has taken huge strides in financial and resource management since 1994. Advances in the areas of cash management, asset management, debt management, labor allocation, and financial reporting have allowed the chamber to move from a financial situation of significant debt—including a $350,000 note, an $800,000 mortgage, and loans of $200,000—to a position of no debt in 1999.

Since 1994, the chamber has seen

- an increase in dues revenue from $1.8 million to $2.4 million;

- interest income, once virtually zero, of $145,000 annually;

- a five-year pledge program for economic development that will be renewed this year with a goal of exceeding $10 million; and

- an increase in grant funding from $0 to $1.5 million.

The history

In 1994, the chamber, with only $16,000, struggled to make payroll. Internal controls were weak and finance staff were inexperienced and isolated from chamber operations and from each other. The association staff focused on presenting the data in a format designed to disguise the chamber's unstable financial position.

The process of change

New staff was added to the chamber's management team in early 1994. Per the board's request, the chamber shifted its focus to revitalization and creating more comprehensive financial and management information. The board knew that demands for scarce cash and staff resources were intensifying, and they were concerned about the chamber's future.

In addition, the infrastructure of the chamber needed attention. In 1995, a new computer system—both hardware and software—was installed. Staff changes were made, and a smaller, more experienced staff was put in place. This not only gave the chamber new expertise, but also decreased operating expenses.

The new staff created and implemented policies and procedures for financial management and operations. Included in the new plan was an advanced time-tracking system developed specifically to coordinate the annual planning process with staff resources and allow the chamber to record true program costs for future analysis. Jacksonville is one of the first Chambers of Commerce to explore and implement full costing at program levels. The system is unique in its ability to capture not only labor hours, but also programs, functions, and a comprehensive planning process.

In 1997, the chamber implemented a full activity-based cost system. Each staff member is required to enter time into the time-tracking database; the information automatically goes to payroll, and pay processing is based on these entries.

Full costing to collect and record all program costs requires three components:

- direct program costs;
- direct labor costs; and
- allocated administrative costs based on direct labor hours.

All staff members enter the time they spend on programs and on administrative and other tasks in the time-tracking system. Using staff hours recorded during the month, the system calculates percentages at three levels:

- program hours to total chamber labor hours;
- program hours to total division hours; and
- program hours to total department hours.

These percentages are applied to monthly expense transactions that have been imported from the general ledger. These expenses represent the labor charged to the division and department levels as well as occupancy and general operating overhead expenses. The system consolidates the data into a single journal entry and saves it to a file for importing back into the general ledger. Full-program cost reporting is now available for analysis.

System design

The association used Microsoft Access to develop the time/costing system, providing a user-friendly environment. Staff is comfortable with it and can easily access reports and transfer data to other platforms. An implementation team composed of staff from all divisions and levels guided the implementation process. Continued training—and communicating the project's progress—have helped the staff embrace the system and celebrate its success.

Today, the chamber recognizes some of the benefits directly attributable to the full-costing project:

- more efficient use of limited resources, particularly staff and cash;
- ability to reallocate time to other programs based on need;

- ability to add, modify, or eliminate programs based on real data and contribution to the chamber's overall plan;
- a more effective management team;
- improved communication, as information is readily available to all staff on a timely basis;
- more accurate systems and processes based on timely operations data;
- growth of unrestricted net assets, from $7,406 in 1994 to $1.2 million; and
- enviable 1999 cash position of $1.6 million—after eliminating all debt.

These benefits have improved the annual strategic planning process as well and have given management a new perspective of the true cost of doing business. The volunteers reviewing the strategic plan and financial statements are better able to evaluate and recommend programs for continued funding.

Strategic planning

Strategic planning incorporates the overall chamber mission into each division, department, and program, complete with goals and measurable objectives. Each quarter, directors prepare reports on program progress and financial status, comparing actual cost to budgeted cost, and provide the information to a team comprising the president and vice presidents of finance and planning.

Full-cost information allows staff to analyze not only the profitability of programs but also the viability the programs have within the community. Of course, because the system was designed as an Access database, anyone skilled in report writing can create a report to meet his or her specific needs.

This flexibility is particularly beneficial to the finance staff as they prepare grant reports, an important new revenue source. Staff can select a grant program and print a report detailing the staff functions and hours worked during the reporting period. The labor cost can be estimated based on a fixed, per-hour rate to retain salary confidentiality.

Summary

The Jacksonville Chamber of Commerce has experienced a full economic cycle, moving from financial instability to fiscal responsibility recognized by community leaders. The chamber operates debt-free, maintains conservative cash reserves, and manages a $7.5 million budget supporting more than 100 programs.

A conservative fiscal plan continues to drive the operation with a smaller, experienced staff committed to an open-team approach of financial reporting. Program managers have sound financial information, enabling them to run efficient and effective programs serving the needs of members and the community.

Revitalizing the Association for Members

By David E. Poisson, CAE

Reprinted from
Marketing Fast Facts,
ASAE newsletter,
September 2000

Attracting and retaining members has always been one of the greatest challenges an association faces. During the past 10 years, the challenge has become even more formidable, especially for organizations dealing with massive consolidation of the industries they represent. One such organization, the Tire Association of North America (TANA), of which I became chief staff executive in 1996, managed to survive a major membership crisis by drastically reducing costs, restructuring, and getting back in touch with its members.

An association in trouble

For most of the years since its founding in 1921, when the association was called The National Tire Dealers and Retreaders Association, TANA drew membership from the thousands of small, independent tire businesses found in communities across the United States. In recent years, however, large retail tire companies began to replace those family-owned stores. The new marketplace had fewer potential members with different needs and expectations. By 1996, the association was out of touch with the North American tire replacement market and badly in need of survival tools.

The association had run a $1 million deficit in 1996—most of it due to losses on its 1996 trade show—and was carrying $1 million in long-term debt. It had been losing membership at an annual rate of 20 percent for each of the preceding five years, and trade show attendance had plummeted to fewer than 2,000 buyers.

TANA was spending so much money on salaries and overhead that it had no funds left for developing member programs and services. Drastic measures were needed to move the association from its inward/downward spiral to a position of strength and growth.

Remaking the association

We began by drastically reducing expenses and revamping the association's internal structure. Outsourcing much of the work formerly done in-house allowed us to cut staff members from 26 to 6. We moved our headquarters from a location where rent was very expensive to a shared office suite. We also closed three satellite offices.

After the interior changes were made, the next step was to restructure the association's governance and policies. The board of directors was reduced from 88 to 36; the executive committee from 18 to 6. This plan was initiated by the board and phased in across three years. The process posed no threat to anyone currently on the board because it targeted the future. The bylaws were amended to provide for the direct election of officers and directors through a democratic process.

A nominating committee was formed and made responsible for coming up with nominations. If, however, someone felt that they would like to be part of the nomination list and they hadn't been considered, they were automatically allowed to be on the list by acquiring signatures from at least 25 people. By not following the traditional method of appointing people from a group of insiders, we made people enthusiastic about serving on the board.

Determined to pay attention to changes in the industry, we opened membership to every company in the North American replacement tire market, not just retail tire dealers. Finally, we adopted a new name and logo that appeared on everything we sponsored, calling attention to the changes in TANA.

Regaining the confidence of the industry

To help increase membership, TANA's major initiatives included

- improving and redesigning the annual trade show;
- developing new publications; and
- establishing personal contact with members.

The trade show had always been the organization's most powerful tool for boosting membership. After examining various options for improving it, we decided to join forces with another association in the automotive aftermarket for a larger exhibition. This agreement gave members access to both associations' show venues for one price while reducing the cost of the show for TANA and the other sponsor.

TANA created three new publications to promote news of our comeback plans to members:

- a biweekly fax newsletter;
- a weekly online version of the newsletter; and
- a bimonthly magazine, *Tire Retailing Today,* dedicated to providing the latest retail strategies for companies in the tire market.

Our crisis had taught us, nearly too late, that to keep members we had to give them something of value and listen to their needs. To help reestablish personal contact with members, I traveled to every state association and dealer meeting I could for eight months. I listened to members' concerns and interests and stressed the value of attending the industry's trade show as a way to benefit from all TANA has to offer.

The three initiatives together were very effective. Members began to contact the association, seeking information about how to run their businesses more profitably. By late 1997, TANA had implemented more than 40 new membership programs.

A revamped association

In the end, we reclaimed our show by tripling attendance. We balanced our budget and retired more than 70 percent of our long-term debt. Membership is growing.

Perhaps the most important lesson we learned is that an association must stay close to its members. Now that we are free of high overhead and a large internal bureaucracy, the association is focusing its efforts on new product development, training programs, and better use of new technology to communicate with members.

A 1990s Investment Success Story Revisited

By Craig Silverio, CAE

Reprinted from

ASSOCIATION

MANAGEMENT,

May 2002

Editor's note: *In the June 1998 issue of* ASSOCIATION MANAGEMENT, *Craig Silverio, CAE, then director of finance for the Packaging Machinery Manufacturers Institute (PMMI), Arlington, Virginia, recounted how his organization bolstered its investment revenues by a staggering 200 percent in only 12 months simply by making the decision "to step outside of its conservative comfort zone" in its investment policy.*

That was a fashionable story line back then. With the dot-com phenomenon soon to reach its apex and the stock market on a seemingly endless upward trajectory, the investment culture, giddy with both the prospect and realization of ever-rising returns, seemed to toss aside some of the most basic of investment tenets, such as that a more aggressive investment strategy means more risk, or that what goes up must come down.

Now that the inevitable downturn in the economic cycle has come (and hopefully gone), ASSOCIATION MANAGEMENT *asked Silverio, now vice president of finance at PMMI, to report on how his organization's reserves have fared—and whether the previously espoused "conservative comfort zone" looks like a more attractive option these days.*

PMMI's reserves, which experienced significant growth from the financial markets in the mid-1990s, were not immune to the market slowdown of 2000 and 2001. But while our returns have suffered in the short term, we have not wavered from our long-term investment strategy.

Since PMMI began investing in stocks in 1994, it has managed an average combined annual return (including both stocks and bonds), net of fees, of 10.3 percent—despite a dismal 2001 return of -12.6 percent. Most importantly, in spite of our 2001 results, the 10.3 percent average return significantly

exceeded the 4–5 percent returns that the institute was receiving from its former policy of *laddering* CDs (buying CDs with different dates of maturity and rolling them over into new CDs once they mature). Starting with an investment base of $7 million in 1994, this translated into hundreds of thousands of dollars in additional investment revenue.

Diversification—with equities on the high side

While PMMI has not wavered on its long-term strategy, it has continued to monitor and, as necessary, adjust it to help ensure long-term growth of the reserve fund. PMMI added a fixed-income manager in 1998 to manage the bond portion of the portfolio. In early 2001, based on concerns that large-capitalization, or large-cap, stocks were overvalued, PMMI added managers to oversee both mid-cap growth and international stocks. Thus far, this move has proven to be a wise one, as both of the new managers provided better returns in 2001 than did the large-cap managers.

Meanwhile, as the reserve fund has grown, PMMI has continued to increase its asset allocation in stocks—all the way up until the time of the economic downturn. In 1998 we increased the stock allocation from 50 percent to 65 percent, and in 2000 we raised it again to 80 percent, where it stands today. The portfolio is rebalanced quarterly to maintain the 80–20 equity-to-fixed-income split; regularly scheduled rebalancing helps ensure that you buy new securities low and sell older securities high.

Incidentally, even after taking into consideration that our strategy is a long-term one, we did not fare all that poorly in the past couple of years, in spite of our 80 percent equities allocation. In 2000 PMMI's net return of 0.7 percent exceeded the market index of –4.2 percent. In 2001, the institute reported a –12.6 percent return, versus the index of –7.7 percent. So, despite the less-than-stellar performance of the financial markets, PMMI managed to hold its own in the marketplace over the two-year period.

An unconventional use of reserves

Our official policy, which is somewhat unusual, is to maintain a reserve fund of 200 percent of annual operating expenses. Admittedly, this rather high percentage is partially attributable to the mere fact that at the time we formulated the policy, we had $20 million in the bank and a $10 million operating budget. Having said that, PMMI has benefited from its reserve fund growth in significant ways beyond mere rainy-day reserve uses. Specifically, the gains from its reserve funds have provided the institute with the capital necessary to become the dominant player for the packaging machinery industry on the Internet. Facing competition from for-profit Internet companies like Verticalnet, Malvern, Pennsylvania, PMMI had the financial resources to capture and retain its space as the place to go on the Internet for packaging machinery. We achieved this by investing $7 million to form a for-profit company (packexpo.com, Falls Church, Virginia). Without a reserve policy focused on long-term growth, this opportunity may have been lost. And PMMI's place as the leading trade association and industry resource for packaging machinery may have suffered, as well.

Our high reserve level allows us flexibility as to how funds can be used. In addition to the more traditional rainy-day uses, these funds can be used for anything from normal operating expenses to launching new business services. In other words, our stated policy leaves it fairly open-ended.

Going forward

While PMMI successfully captured the benefits of the surging stock market in the mid- and late-1990s, the institute always recognized that its reserve policy is a *long-term strategy*. So, other than some minor changes in stock diversification, PMMI has chosen to stay the course with respect to its asset allocation of stocks and bonds. Despite the recent economic downturn, it is unlikely that the institute would have done anything differently, as its investment strategy is based on proven, long-term investment principles. Yes, there will be some short-term peaks and valleys in performance. Yet even the events of September 11, 2001, did not create a need to react rashly. Past events, from the Cuban Missile Crisis to the Persian Gulf War and Oklahoma City bombing, did little to disrupt the markets beyond short-term market volatility.

PMMI constantly reviews its investment strategy to make sure that it is aligned with current economic trends. PMMI staff and its investment adviser keep a pulse on the economic environment and report to the board's finance committee annually. Despite recent diversification into mid-cap and international sectors, PMMI's portfolio still has significant exposure to large-cap growth and value stocks. The institute may eliminate or further reduce one of those sectors, based on the belief that near-term growth will continue to come from smaller companies.

Beyond that, the institute's current reserves, approximately $12 million, are well positioned to participate in future waves of market growth. And we move forward with an investment strategy that, once fashionable, is now commonplace.

The 10 Biggest Mistakes We Made Managing Change...and the Lessons We Learned

By Carol Kinsey Goman

Reprinted from
ASAE Global Link,
ASAE newsletter,
June 2000

I've been a professional speaker on the human side of organizational change for 15 years. I've addressed audiences in 17 countries; I've worked with hundreds of executives, managers, and communicators in dozens of industries—and I've seen firsthand how the management (and the mismanagement) of change impacts a work force. From my perspective, here are the 10 biggest mistakes that we've made managing change—and the lessons we've learned.

1. **We didn't understand the importance of people.** Sixty to 70 percent of all restructuring failed—not because of strategy, but because of the "human dimension." Michael Hammer, author of *Reengineering the Corporation,* says, "I wasn't smart enough about people. I was reflecting my engineering background and was insufficiently appreciative of the human dimension. I've learned that's critical."

   Lesson learned: Organizations don't change. People do—or they don't. If the human beings in your organization don't trust leadership, don't share the organization's vision, don't buy into the reason for change, and aren't included in the planning, there will be no successful change—regardless of how brilliant your strategy is.

2. **We expected that people throughout the organization would have similar reactions to change.**

   Lesson learned: Some people in an organization are naturally more change-adept. We need to spot and encourage the early adapters—and we need to develop change-adept employee profiles to better understand how to develop these qualities throughout the organization.

3. **We treated transformation as an event rather than a mental, physical, and emotional process.** Lacking emotional literacy, we disregarded the wrenching emotional process of large-scale change—and when we began to address the emotional component, we underestimated its depth.

   Lesson learned: Leaders of change must become proficient at facilitating the emotional process of change. There are five stages in the transformation process: denial, resistance, choice, acceptance, and commitment. Different management strategies are effective in addressing the various emotions in each of these stages.

4. **We presented the current change effort as the answer to the future.** Then, when subsequent changes were announced, they were viewed with skepticism and distrust.

   Lesson learned: There is no single solution for the future. No one can predict or control the tyrannies of global markets, societal pressures, government regulations, technological advances, and customer demands that shape the future. We must develop resilient work forces capable of committing to the current change strategy, while staying alert to the conditions that signal the need to alter our course.

5. **We were less than candid.** Under the rationale of protecting people, we presented change with a too positive spin. And the more we sugar-coated the truth, the wider the trust gap grew between management and the work force.

   Lesson learned: Communicate honestly. Today's employees are demanding it. Not everyone will thank you for your candor, but they will never forgive you for anything less.

6. **We did a poor job of setting the stage for change.** All too often change was announced in an environmental vacuum, with little reason or rationale for what the organization was trying to accomplish and how this change fit into the corporate vision.

   Lesson learned: To prepare employees for success in a rapidly changing business environment, we must give them pertinent information about demographic, global, economic, technological, competitive, and industry trends. People need to know the vision, goals, and strategy of the company. They need to understand the financial reality of the business and how their actions impact that reality.

7. **We tried to manage transformation with the same strategies used for incremental change.**

   Lesson learned: Incremental change—continual improvement, and so forth—is linear, predictable, logical, and based on a progressive acceleration of past performance. Transformation is none of these things. Transformation is a redefinition of who we are and what we do. It's often unpredictable (responding to unforeseen circumstances, challenges, and opportunities), illogical (demanding people and organizations change when they are the most successful), and most importantly, in a

transformative change, our past success is not a valid indicator of future success. In fact, our past success may be our greatest obstacle.

8. **When the corporate culture changed from one of entitlement, we forgot to negotiate the new compact between employers and employees.** The result was that people knew what they were losing, but didn't have a clear picture of what to expect in its place.

   Lesson learned: Employee commitment is still a vital element of successful organizations, but an entirely new compact between employer and employee is required. This new understanding moves the organizational mindset from paternalism to vibrant partnerships. The new compact must be conscious, realistic, and mutual.

9. **We believed that change-communication was what employees heard or read from corporate headquarters.** So we focused our attention on speeches, newsletters, videos, and e-mail—only to find out that, from an employee's perspective, the kind of communication that impacts behavior is 10 percent traditional vehicles, 45 percent organizational structure (whatever punishes or rewards), and 45 percent management behavior.

   Lesson learned: A communication strategy that is not congruent with organizational systems and the actions of leadership are useless. In the words of one CEO, "What you do in the hallways is more important than what you say in the meeting."

10. **This final mistake was our worst mistake.** We underestimated human potential. And when we underestimated potential, we wasted it.

    Lesson learned: Trust in the innate intelligence, capability, and creativity of your employees—and people will astound you. As the head of quality at Motorola put it, "We never envisioned that well-empowered people at even the lowest, entry-level positions, properly trained within their skill levels, could move heaven and earth."

Selected Resources

From ASAE:

The following books can be ordered from ASAE's Member Service Center at 202-371-0940, or from ASAE's Online Bookstore at http://www.asaenet.org/bookstore.

Managing Association Turnarounds
By Charles E. Bartling, CAE, 1997. (ASAE Product Number: 216786)

Outsourcing: Using Outside Resources To Get More Done
By Stacey Riska, 2001. (ASAE Product Number: 216824)